THE
HOUSE and COTTAGE
HANDBOOK

stone and harling—Tweedmouth, Northumberland

This book is sponsored by FERGUSON INDUSTRIAL HOLDINGS LIMITED of Appleby Castle, Cumbria, to enable the publication of a simple handbook on the aesthetics of improving and converting old cottages and houses, for all those considering or about to embark on such a venture

THE
HOUSE
AND
COTTAGE
HANDBOOK

NEVILLE WHITTAKER
Foreword by Sir John Summerson
CBE BA FSA RIBA

Civic Trust for the North East

Published by the
CIVIC TRUST FOR THE NORTH EAST,
34/35 Saddler Street, Durham

First published 1976
Second Edition 1977
© 1976 Neville Whittaker

Printed in England by the
Hindson Print Group Ltd.,
Newcastle upon Tyne NE99 1PO

ISBN: 0 905516 00 1

CONTENTS

Whitfield Place, Wolsingham, County Durham; a late 17th-century Manor House, recently restored.

FOREWORD

Among Ruskin's many pronouncements about the preservation of old buildings is one which sticks in my mind because of its poignant, if rather whimsical, logic. In it he develops the argument that the destruction of old work is, in a special sense, waste of time. Here is how he puts it:

You allow it to be wrong to waste your own time; but then it must be still more wrong to waste other people's; for you have some right to your own time, but none to theirs. Well, then if it is thus wrong to waste the time of the living, it must be still more wrong to waste the time of the dead; for the living can redeem their time, the dead cannot. But you waste the best time of the dead when you destroy the works they have left you; for to those works they gave the best of their time, intending them for immortality.

The passage contains the idea of heritage and also the idea of building for permanence. I do not think for a moment that Ruskin would have hesitated to pull down every speculative villa within a hundred miles of his home at Denmark Hill; villas which, being leasehold, were not meant to last more than ninety-nine years. What he believed was that the older traditions of building were not conditioned by such sordid economics and did in fact embody the sentiment we associate with the word 'heritage'. To a great extent, he was right.

Today we would probably wish to extend Ruskin's notion of good building even to some of the speculative work of his day and up to our own. Really good bricklaying, masonry, carpentry and joinery, whenever found and whenever executed is precious stuff and becoming more precious as building becomes increasingly industrialised. Of course we sometimes have to get rid of it but Ruskin's point—and the ground theme of this book—is that we should never do so needlessly and without thought.

To act rightly in this matter is not easy. The first thing we need to do is to learn to recognise good traditional craft methods when we see them and in this the chapters which follow should be of great use and, I think, should give a new incentive to exploring the countryside; investigating not only the conspicuously historic buildings but all which catch the eye as being agreeable. Or, indeed, disagreeable; for taste and knowledge in these things come from comparing. Furthermore, if we believe that our building heritage is something worth cherishing we must look deeper than the merely photogenic character of the buildings we appreciate. We must be aware of the nature of their materials and of how they were put together.

To those responsible for the maintenance and alteration of old houses this book is specially addressed. Dealing sympathetically with these things is difficult and I welcome the section which explains the architect's role and is frank about what his assistance may run you into. It may well cost less than running into trouble and spoiling a good home.

But the main message of this book is the very simple one enunciated so delicately by Ruskin. Never destroy good old work unless you must. Do not waste the time of the dead.

John Summerson

May 1976

HOUSE AND COTTAGE

This book is about old houses and what we do to them. Most of the examples shown are from the northern counties of England but the message and the moral is national. Our stock of old houses, whether they are rural cottages, terraces of orderly Victorian and Edwardian houses in our towns, a row of pit cottages, an isolated farmhouse or whatever, are a national asset economically, visually and historically. What we are doing to this national asset, our traditional or vernacular background of buildings, is not always of the best.

In aiming to show some of the ways old houses can be dealt with sympathetically and with care and understanding, this book is perhaps too dogmatic. There are naturally exceptions to every rule, but in the main the simple dictum of the landscapists, to stop, look and 'observe the genius of the place' should apply to every subject for improvement well before the first ideas are committed to paper.

It seems that almost everyone has a dream of a cottage in the country, or of using some of this country's splendid stock of older houses as a basis for a family home. As a nation we have, of recent years, come to appreciate the value of utilising fully this stock, of improving these houses and bringing them up to the environmental standards we nowadays expect. This in turn gives to these buildings a new lease of life, and should, ideally, enable their continuance as part of the scenery and general environment which we know and love. This is therefore a happy prospect for through this process many good buildings will be retained which would otherwise disappear; houses and cottages brought back to life from dereliction, closing orders and the brink of destruction.

Happily, many of these improvements, alterations and modernisations are well and carefully considered and do just that. A great many do not. The crude, brash, illiterate so called improvements which are applied in too many cases are more destructive in the end than outright demolition. In many cases it might have been better to start again completely.

Change is an inevitable part of our everyday surroundings of buildings; the very nature of building materials and the building's construction ensures this. Roofs invariably need replacing before the walls; doors and windows are relatively easy and inexpensive to alter, whilst changes in health standards and living requirements suggest a whole variety of alteration both inside and out. Change then is not only inevitable, it is desirable. This is not contended, the problems stem from the type and scale of changes.

In the past, changes and additions occurred at relatively infrequent intervals, giving time for new features and fashions to be absorbed into 'tradition' and the landscape. New techniques of construction and fabrication were absorbed into the repertoire of the provincial mason, joiner and designer very slowly, and often passed through successive generations to reach ultimate refinement. The sash window, introduced to this country from Holland around 1700 was almost immediately accepted, and was only finally rejected for mass housing in the first quarter of our own century. During this time however it had changed in size, proportion, refinement and pattern of glazing.

Today, change is fast and often untried. The manufacturers of building components, advertise and market a vast range. The 'do it yourselfer' or the local builder can buy, off the peg, almost anything. Fashion and whim enables us to Georgianise or 'Regencyfy' at the drop of a hat. Just as the plastic surgeon can change our faces dramatically, so we can change our houses and convert what was a simple straightforward artisans dwelling in some provincial town into some neo-Georgian dream or nightmare, depending upon our point of view and standard of taste. We are rapidly becoming past masters of the phoney.

This fact is clearly emphasised by a personal return to towns and villages known and remembered from past years. Fond recollections are crudely shattered by the changes which have occurred in the intervening period. We tend to be oblivious to the slow changes in our immediate environment and it is only by stepping back that we can fully appreciate their cumulative implications. The heart of the town or village is perhaps still much the same, some houses well improved, some disfigured in the process. Around the town are the rash of boxes in whatever superficial style is currently 'in' and almost every old farmhouse, cottage or other dwelling 'improved' in the half-remembered ambience of either a Costa Brava holiday or from a random selection from any manufacturers catalogue. What is almost totally absent is honesty of treatment, sympathy and understanding.

This book is not designed to stem the natural process of change but to suggest that care and knowledge should be applied to the improvement of older properties in order that the qualities of these buildings, often the very things which attracted the owner in the first place, may be retained and enhanced.

Many still hold the belief that the home is the Englishman's true castle and that he should be free to do with it whatsoever he likes. Indeed the very properties now under concern were created in the days before the planning machine came into existence. Very little really in the way of statutory requirements is put in the way of the would-be 'improver', but this is often compounded by a manifest insensitivity and lack of understanding of the basic qualities of the initial building. To an extent this is understandable in that there is very little written of direct help and assistance.

It might well be argued that no one has the right to set him or herself up as an arbiter of taste or fashion. History clearly shows that fashion and ideas are constantly changing. Today, recent architecture is looked upon somewhat askance, whilst the formality and order of Georgian architecture is regarded with admiration. Attitudes were very different in the late nineteenth century. We will certainly experience yet another about turn. The basis of this book is that alterations should be in keeping with the essential character of the building and its immediate neighbourhood. It aims to show what changes can be effected that will provide the necessary level of improvement whilst enhancing actual appearance. Unfortunately this is not a view shared by all. A letter written to a provincial paper some time ago criticised the attempts of the Planning Department to control the proliferation of mass produced bow windows in one village. It argued that 'Only a Planning Department would have the gall to try to dictate on a matter of opinion such as windows. What does it matter if bow windows are mock Georgian and how can they be sure that any they propose wouldn't be mock something or other, or do they intend fossilising one particular style or age? Any display of free expression is just what this country needs, and thank goodness the planners do not have the power to control this freedom'.

This letter somewhat misses the point. In criticising the type of 'improvements' which are occurring across the country, it is not sought to stultify flair and individuality nor to try to produce a sterile uniformity. The aim is to try to aid an appreciation of scale and style in context. It is an attempt to stall the incongrous and to prevent really major indiscretions which represent a sad blot on the landscape. With a little knowledge and understanding on everyone's part the 'gall' would not have been necessary.

This problem is not an isolated one and there is no personal, no individual villain. It results from an inadequacy of information. Most of the alterations dealt with in this book are classified as 'Permitted Development' and are therefore largely outside statutory control. There is little influence possible from the planners and the situation is aggravated by the fact that Building Regulations are often at variance with desirable aesthetic standards. In addition there is the effect on taste and style advocated by some magazines aimed at the 'do it yourselfer' and the would-be improver. Some changes and alterations are truly bad in this age let alone any other. Finally, there is the problem of copying bad examples. The resulting combination of these factors is a conspiracy of ignorance and the creation of almost total disasters in the name of improvement.

The situation could be very different with a little more care, a little knowledge and a great deal more sensitivity. This is what this book is about. It is not a complicated history of vernacular building but a simple attempt to induce thought and respect in the hope that would-be improvers will stop, think and try to understand before they act. Perhaps, as has been said, it is too dogmatic and that its reasoning does not universally apply. If, however, it goes some way to help those about to start work and to aid the continuance of the great heritage of lesser building then its purpose will be fulfilled.

The vernacular basis—an unimproved stone and pantile farmhouse, County Durham

Mid 19th-century stone and slate terrace house, with contemporary sash windows and door

The house Georgianised; the proportions changed with bar-divided casement windows and bow and an off-the-peg doorcase

Above: A usual subject for the improver—a farmhouse now surplus to requirements
Below: The changes in terrace housing can be more devastating—one house can spoil a whole terrace

BASIC PRINCIPLES AND AIMS

It has been said that the face of a house is the face of the man for whom it was built. There are those straight forward and honest, those decorative and amusing, those elaborate and pompous and the phoney and dubious. All are the faces of houses and of people we meet every day. The older houses of this country may be basic shelters designed to meet the needs of a primitive life, rural cottages or lines of terrace houses in our industrial towns; they may be more imposing dwellings, Victorian or Georgian Vicarages and Rectories or Edwardian villas, or really grand structures reflecting the whim of passing fashion and the hand of the architect.

In the nothern counties, vernacular building is not much in evidence from before the sixteenth century, although there are a few isolated earlier domestic buildings—pele towers which were subsequently converted, medieval manors and the like. After the turmoil and unrest of the middle ages, the seventeenth century at last brought some measure of prosperity and security, particularly in the fertile agricultural lands and the upland sheep-rearing areas, which resulted in a century of widespread reconstruction and new building. Although the new ideas of the Renaissance were being introduced, they were poorly understood, and deep in the dales, people clung to the old traditions and methods of design right through the century. This phase of growth and building continued throughout the eighteenth century and produced the seeds of development of the major towns. The chief characteristics of much eighteenth-century domestic architecture were, simple rectangular compositions, severe classical cornices and pediments—which became highly-important features in towns like Stokesley in North Yorkshire—the minimum of decoration and well-proportioned sash windows. In more elaborate designs these were surrounded and surmounted by classical mouldings, but in the simpler farmhouses and cottages they had plain stone architraves and robust decoration. It was, by and large, a respectable architecture, dignified and unpretentious.

A few serious attempts at co-ordinated architectural planning outside the towns were made, notably villages like Lowther in Cumbria and Blanchland in Northumberland. Long terraces and crescents were constructed but were only to be found in important towns.

Only after the Napoleonic Wars and with the fruits of industrialisation becoming evident did vernacular architecture change in both scale and type. Brick, stone and stucco terraces of houses in the towns and the first industrial ter-

Shape and massing are important. Later extensions to this farmhouse have created a sympathetic long low group. County Durham

13

Above left: Handsomely proportioned early 18th-century brick farmhouse. North Yorkshire. 'Architecture' is now evident in the baroque door and case, the stepped arched lintols and the projecting centre bay with small pediment

Above right: High and handsome North Yorkshire farmhouse, slightly later in date and now with stone quoins and string courses. Note the elaborate doorcase and the thick glazing bars in both examples

Left: Late 18th-century flint and cobble house. East Anglia. Note the window dressings now in brick and the pantile roof usual through much of eastern England and Scotland

The variety of domestic vernacular is endless
Above left: Slate cottage with slate string courses, circular chimney and
*   roof. Troutbeck, Cumbria*
Above right: Brick and pantile cottages with handsome sash and Gothic
*   windows. Humberside*
Right: 17th-century brick and stone cottages. Burneston, North
*   Yorkshire. Note the classical pediments to the windows carried out in*
*   brickwork, the stone frames and mullions, the stone quoins and the*
*   half-stone walling*

races in what hitherto had been open countryside began to appear. The enclosure of the common lands and the uplands resulted in the growth of further farmsteads and small-holdings. Much of the more sophisticated development was in the then fashionable Greek style, popularised by the newly emerging provincial architects in cities like Newcastle, Nottingham and Hull. Curiously, this particular vogue had a long life in the northern counties, lasting well into the second half of the nineteenth century, and was exemplified by Doric and Ionic porches, 'Grecian' mouldings around windows and cornices, although these were carried out in the tough stone and stucco of the North. There has always been a considerable 'time gap' between the North country and the South.

Playful and amusing architecture is perhaps best exemplified by the Gothick domestic building of the second half of the eighteenth century. Happily, examples of this are by no means uncommon, even though the style may only appear in single elements such as the tall staircase windows of many houses. The new Gothick was a lighthearted decorative style, endearing in its cheerful disregard of the true nature of Gothic building, in the ingenuity of the results, and was extremely fashionable in the North country.

The nineteenth century proper is most commonly associated with the long rows of brick terrace houses and cottages of the industrial revolution. They were both simple and economical in construction, and in their day often provided much improved standards of accommodation and sanitation. Also, beginning as single rows, they only sank to the endless monotony of the rapidly-growing terraces through unimaginative repetition. Much of this housing was more enlightened than modern predjudices allow us to admit, and even today with careful treatment these houses can provide good standard basic housing.

In looking at suitable 'subjects for improvement', we are most likely to be seeking simple structures of traditional material and form which can be extended in some way, or for larger, perhaps even rambling houses, which call for either subdivision or reduction in size. Other possibilities are the straightforward improvements to subjects like the middle class terrace houses of suitable family size available in most of our towns, or of buildings never before used for domestic purposes—chapels, churches, barns, schools, warehouses and mills.

In all these cases, there are basic principles which should never be lost to sight in the scramble to get the works underway or to try to meet ever-rising costs and the mass of necessary statutory procedures.

(a) Try first to assess something of the history of the building and the various past changes to it. What items or character drew you to it in the first place? If it was the comfortable sense of enclosure, then it would be senseless to discover at some later date that you 'must' provide more daylight, larger windows and all; the initial response to the character of the place would be lost. If it was the warm mellow glow of the old brickwork or the pattern and patina of the clay pantile roof which drew you, then all would be lost if you had to replace this because of costs with a harsh cement rendering or a new roof of concrete tile. Do not therefore lose sight of your original reactions and objectives.

(b) How is the building 'massed'—is it a long low building under one continous roof or is it a mixture of gables, valleys and ridges. Whatever it is should indicate the form of any extension. Importantly, look at neighbouring buildings; is there general uniformity of ridge and eaves heights, and would a dramatic change in this make or mar the overall quality of the group. To provide 'sore thumbs' to stick out is no-one's aim.

(c) Aim always for the highest standards in design and quality available within the limits of your purse. If you aim to keep in 'keeping'—to insert new Georgian sash windows or a new porch, then these have to be 'right'. Nothing looks worse, or more naive, than ill understood, illiterate period detailing.

If you are in any doubt as to what is required, look at one or more of the many books now available of period details. Do not think that everything has to be 'of a piece' and of one style. In the past, additions and alterations were made in the fashion of their day. A new extension or a conversion can be unashamedly modern, provided that the standard of the design is high and that it respects what is already there.

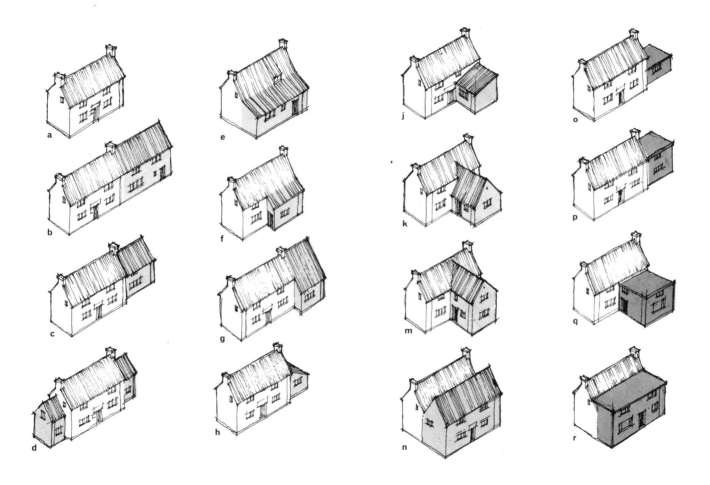

Appropriate ways to extend the simple rectangular house (a); by extending in length—a usual traditional way (b); by a smaller subordinate extension in length (c); or two symmetrical wings (d). More usual cottage extensions are in the form of a single-storey rear block under the same roof (e); a smaller version (f); an end extension emphasising the roof and creating an 'L' shaped plan (g); and a small end outshot under a lean-to-roof (h)

Rear extensions can take the form of a small mono pitched roof wing (j); a single-storey gabled extension (k); or a gabled extension of two storeys (m). In the past houses were often doubled in size by the addition of a new block of the same size with a central valley roof. This creates an almost square plan form (n). Unsympathetic extensions ignore the roof shape of the original building at either one storey (c); or two (p). Rear wings can be very ungainly (q); or fit badly to the existing roof shape (r)

Traditional facing come in many forms; stucco rendering or 'harling' over stone or brick (a); brickwork with hand- or machine-made brick (b); and the many varieties of masonry—coursed rubble (c); tooled coarse ashlar (d); and traditional upland rubble masonry (e)

WALLS AND FINISHES

Although the plan forms of cottages and houses vary widely, they were almost always constructed from the materials closest to hand. Thus, although pressed earth, cob and pisé, and timber framing are common in some parts of these islands, they are rare or totally absent in others. The association of timber-framed construction with counties such as Shropshire, Cheshire, Kent and Sussex is amply evident. Nevertheless the use of timber framing in conjunction with 'mass' walling—stone and brick, in elements like the 'cruck' frame appears almost everywhere in traditional construction. There are numerous examples in North Yorkshire and County Durham.

The materials most commonly encountered are brick and stone. The colour, texture and workability of native stones varies, and it is from these inherent qualities that an areas vernacular springs. The red sandstones of Cumbria are coarse and relatively difficult to work and certainly to carve. Hence a traditional architecture arose of simple shapes and with little ornamentation. The brittle slate of the Lake District lends itself readily to the type of walling associated with that area and the architectural exploitation of the material. The basic character of masonry is derived from the shapes of the component stones; whether these can be easily worked and dressed and how it is done; and also the way in which they are joined and pointed. There is in every stone area a local idiom of working and of technique of construction which should be carefully observed; sometimes small pebbles and stones were inserted into the wide joints of irregular masonry, this is known as 'galletting' though it is rarely found in the North; various types of surface dressing are related to a particular area and stone, the chevron dressing pattern on the ironstone of Cleveland is a good example of this.

Weather and atmospheric conditions bring wear and texture to natural stone. The problem is not to eradicate this process but to prevent further decay. Note the traditional course of stone slab to this pantile roof at the eaves

Stone dressed to a smooth finish and set with fine joints, ashlar, was generally reserved for grander buildings, though even smaller houses occasionally incorporate ashlar on the principal facade. More usually, ashlar was reserved for selected elements, string courses, quoins, cornices, the tabling to gables, window and door surrounds and chimneys, the rest being executed in coursed but irregular masonry. Many of the traditional details, associated with these elements in the building, date from the seventeenth century, and should be studied before they are either replaced or repaired. The Dales, both in the West and North Ridings of Yorkshire, contain numerous examples of these details, whilst occasionally, very local patterns can be found, e.g. the volutes, forming the kneeling stones on gables· are a feature of the local architecture of Berwick-upon-Tweed.

Great care must be taken to match new masonry to old. This is not easy. Older walls are generally of solid masonry, whilst new work is little more than an outer facing to the cavity and inner leaf of brick or block.

Whilst stone was an ancient and widely-used material, except in the east and south-east of England, brick was to become the common material, except in the uplands of the Pennines and the North West. To a certain extent before the great industrial expansion of the nineteenth century, the areas of general brick use complemented the areas of stone. Although some medieval brick survives, its first introduction was at Hull in the fourteenth century, most brickwork encountered, dates from the eighteenth and nineteenth centuries. All of this was locally produced, transport costs were high until the coming of the railways, and it afforded a relatively quick and easy method of construction.

At first brick was regarded as a costly but beautiful alternative to stone. Bricks were handmade up to the first half of the nineteenth century. The early bricks are thinner than modern bricks, and because they were handmade and the clays were not as thoroughly prepared as modern standards permit, the bricks distorted in shape when baked and vary considerably in overall dimensions. To allow them to be walled satisfactorily, they were generally set with very wide mortar joints. Thus old brickwork has an attractive quality produced by the proportion of brick face to joint and the texture and pattern produced by distortion and variations of colour. Where these qualities exist, they should be carefully safeguarded.

Both old brickwork and masonry can be spoiled by careless repointing which spills over on to the face of the materials. Old brickwork was generally pointed with a soft lime mortar mix.

The introduction of patterned brickwork dates from Tudor times, but remained a vernacular survival until the middle of the nineteenth century when it again became architecturally fashionable. Patterns derived from using two colours of brick are an interesting facade feature of houses in several Northern country towns.

The use of soft, rubbing brick, which could be shaped afterwards by hand for arched openings and ornamentation dates from the first quarter of the eighteenth century, although this also became a feature of the revived 'Queen Anne' style of the last years of the nineteenth century.

It is very difficult to match up modern bricks satisfactorily to old work. Modern surface patterns—sand facings, wire cutting, etc., never look well right alongside the old. It may still be possible to obtain second-hand handmade bricks reclaimed from some demolition—they clean easily because of the soft mortar generally used—or try to obtain new handmade bricks. Unhappily the number of works producing these has declined rapidly in recent years, but they are still obtainable. An alternative possibility is to use some of the narrow machine-made slot-moulded bricks now being produced. These match up satisfactorily to old brickwork and they too look well set with thick joints.

Harder, machine-made bricks, introduced during the nineteenth century vary widely in colour, texture and quality. They form the mass of general domestic building. Variations in colour, sometimes present in cheaper bricks, especially those produced in conjunction with the coal mining industry, can help to produce an attractive result.

During the first half of the nineteenth century, when exposed brickwork had fallen from fashion, stucco rendering, in imitation of stone—even sometimes marked with stone joints—was widely used to cover other materials, brick and even stone itself. Stucco rendering had been in general use, for over a century before, both as a decorative finish and to provide further weather protection. Particular local traditions existed. Some areas like Cumbria contain many such early nineteenth-century buildings, in the Lake District and in small areas such as Dentdale in Yorkshire. What sometimes appears as rendering is the build up of lime wash over many generations. Traditional Scottish 'harling', generally seen in the East, is an integral part of the local vernacular. The finish of the rendering is very important. Too often it can look very hard and uncompromising—all very well on a later house with some grandeur, but inappropriate on a small rural cottage. The use of a wooden float to provide the finish on rendering can produce a soft texture which looks well with older buildings. Regular or contrived patterns, except perhaps those in the manner of East Anglian pargetting, should be avoided. Modern techniques of pebble dash or Tyrolean finish look too regular and harsh for old buildings.

A useful Scots technique, often used in the Northern Counties, is to form quasi jambs, heads and cills around openings in stucco, changing the texture of the finish from the roughness of the wall surface to a smooth finish for these surrounds.

Some comment should be made on other wall finishing techniques which might be encountered. Horizontal overlapping boarding—weather board, is really only traditional to the East and South East, associated perhaps most directly with the clapboard cottages of Kent. Modern versions of this boarding in aluminium, hardwood, redwood or other timber treated with preservative—required now by the Building Regulations—are in general use on new buildings, but are somewhat inappropriate to the conversion of older houses. They could be used to good effect on extensions and it is often better to change the surfacing material completely than to effect an unsatisfactory match. The sections of these elements are however generally too large in scale to be totally satisfactory. Smaller sections of hardwood boarding might be useful on smaller parts of the building, such as the cheeks of dormer windows or insert panels.

Vertically hung tile, either plain or patterned mathematical tiles—sometimes known as mechanical tiles, are strictly native to the East and South East. They are intended as an outer, impermeable, skin to timber-framed building. Their use as decorative elements for mass housing today like the use of vertically hung slate in small panels is really without much traditional basis. Slate was hung over large stretches of walling in areas like the Lake District, usually to provide extra cover and protection to very exposed gables.

The use of large cobbles for walling appears in several areas; in the North around Hornsea in Humberside, the Solway Firth and North West Lancashire. This can be very decorative.

The walls of any house make up one of the chief visual elements of that house and can, if carelessly or unsympathetically treated with bad pointing, hard rendering, or the poor matching or introduction of new materials, change drastically the appearance of the house. Again approach the problems with care and understanding; try to keep materials which have weathered attractively and where these are disfigured by dirt and grime, surface cleaning may be the answer.

Where rendering has to be replaced during restoration or where it is being applied for the first time, great care should be taken in deciding the surface pattern. Results can be dramatic and not always what is expected

Above: Farmhouse near Richmond, North Yorkshire before and after the replacement of rendering

Left: Successive generations of limewash creates a hard skin not unlike render. Settle, North Yorkshire

Above: Before and after colourwashing brickwork, the street entrance to a town cottage in Durham City
   Architects: Samson Jones, South Shields
Right: The dramatic effect of new rendering in a Victorian terrace improvement at Wallsend, Tyne and Wear
   Architects: Owen Luder and Brian Jones, Newcastle upon Tyne

ROOFS
AND ROOF FINISHES

Roofs were invariably designed to accommodate one particular finish, generally native to that area and therefore easily obtained. The choice was also determined by the ease with which the covering material could be used—were the tiles or slabs easily cut or mitred, and the pitch right to prevent rain penetration. Obvious examples were the low pitch of the heavy, stone slabs of the uplands, laid with large overlaps and the relatively lightweight pantile roofs of the eastern areas with very little overlap thus requiring a much steeper pitch.

The methods and techniques of roofing in turn dictated the shape of the building—whether there were projections requiring smaller gables, and valleys, or whether the roof finish enabled the roof to be 'hipped'. Only with the adoption of the flat roof has a totally free plan form become possible. Some forms were traditional, the gabled two-storey house extended at the rear by a one-storey extension, all contained beneath one continuous roof, called, in the North, a 'catslide', whilst others in the use of projecting bays and gables, followed current fashion. Generally, plain tile and thatch were easier to form into valleys and hips than slate and pantile—a difficult material to cut properly, although there are many examples of hipped pantile roofs. Some materials were of ancient origin, whilst others, the Welsh blue slates for example, were introduced later in time and are the mark of a particular phase of traditional building.

Thatch is perhaps the most ancient of all roofing materials, though not much now survives in the North, except in isolated pockets; North Northumberland, the area around the Solway Firth and in parts of Yorkshire. Most of this was straw thatch, although many upland houses were thatched with ling and heather. In almost all cases it has been replaced by Norfolk or imported reed thatch and in many more cases by the stopgap of corrugated iron.

Roofing slabs of stone are generally confined to the upland areas of the Pennines, though stone tiles are a feature of vernacular architecture of the Cotswolds, North East Cheshire and the midland counties such as parts of south Lincolnshire, Northamptonshire and Leicestershire.

The heavy slabs of the Pennines are of great size and weight and hence require a sturdy roof structure to support them and are laid generally at pitch of 30° or less. Because they were laid with large overlaps, course to course, they are resistent to driving rain and snow even at such a low pitch. The slabs were fixed to the roofing battens with oak pegs or occasionally sheep bones, and the two chief causes for their decay are the slipping of the slabs due to the failure of the pegs or from the weathering of the stone on the underside of the slabs. Slabs from old roofs can sometimes be re-used, but generally, unless they are carefully selected, this is not recommended. Concrete slabs with a stone finish have been available for some time and are a passable substitute though these cannot look other than just that. Natural stone slabs are usually graded from large slabs at the eaves to small slabs at the ridge.

A common roofing tradition in parts of the North was to use three or four courses of heavy stone slab at the eaves of pantile roofs. This allowed a firmer setting at the vulnerable eaves line and helped to prevent wind lift of tiles at this point. It is an attractive touch.

The undersides of stone slab roofs were 'torched', that is, pointed with mortar to prevent rain penetration, although this often fails and the mortar falls into the roof space.

Smaller stone tiles were generally laid to a much steeper pitch, 50° or more, and because they were small in size were capable of being 'swept' in valleys and around hips.

Plain clay tiles are the most common of roof finishes in the Eastern and South Eastern counties, but occur rarely in traditional building in the North. They are clearly related to the brick manufacturing areas. Today they are widely used in new work or replacements, but like brick the differences in quality and texture between the old handmade tiles, varied and irregular in shape though not in overall size, and the new mass-produced standardised tiles, is considerable. Like stone slabs they are laid with a considerable overlap—each tile overlaps two others in lower courses—and are fixed with nails and the nibs which appear on the underside of the tiles.

They were generally laid at a pitch of 45° and over.

Clay pantiles, like plain tiles are usually found in the Eastern counties but are common in Eastern Scotland and Northern England. They are a development of the half-round Latin tile, incorporating what is virtually a double roll. The size of pantiles, like plain tiles, was fixed during the eighteenth century, though they appeared, imported from the Low Countries, during the late seventeenth century.

Pantiles are a lightweight roof covering, with very little lap between courses. This is made possible because of a side overlap, not available in plain tiles. Although they can be laid to a low pitch of 30°, they serve best when the pitch is much steeper, and appear so in traditional work. The steep pitch helps to prevent rain penetration between the small overlaps. Their lightweight enables the roof structure to be both lighter and cheaper.

Today, clay pantiles are still available and should be used in the restoration or replacement of pantiled roofs. More modern developments such as glazed-finish pantiles or double Roman tiles should generally be avoided. Clay pantiles have not only a beautiful rich colour but weather quickly and gracefully. The deep indentations of the overall roof surface in the traditional pantile shape give a rich texture and pattern to the roof both in sunshine and shade.

Pantiles are difficult to cut and form satisfactorily and hence are generally used on gabled roofs only though there are some notable exceptions with hips, dormers, etc., in both ancient and Edwardian roofs. The pantiles were almost always 'torched' on the underside to prevent water penetration.

One of the great disadvantages of clay pantile in traditional form is that when the torching failed and fell away and there was some movement in the tiles perhaps through high winds, and age, there was the inevitable penetration of the roof by water and snow. Torching can now be replaced by the use of boarding or felting or plastic sheeting beneath the battens under the tiles. Many roofs have been spoiled in appearance by the replacement of clay pantile roofs with more modern roofing materials with less relief and pattern but with the undoubted advantage of better protection.

Slate is naturally found only in relatively-small areas of these islands; North Wales, North Lancashire and Cumbria, Cornwall and Devon. The colour of slate and its consistency varies considerably from the blue slates of North Wales, hard and brittle and capable of being riven (split) into wafer-thin pieces, to the blue and blue-green slates of the Burlington quarries and Coniston, and to the lighter green slates of Kirkstone. Generally, the slates of the Lake District are thicker and more friable. Lake District slate is laid in diminishing courses from eaves to ridge, whereas, Welsh slate is used in thin pieces of uniform thickness and size. All slates are laid at pitches of about 30–35°.

With the coming of the railways and the possibility of cheap transportation of slate from the quarries of North Wales coupled with the burgeoning of the new towns of the Industrial Revolution, slate became the commonest roofing material of the nineteenth century, both for new building and in the replacement of older roofs, though now it is no longer easy to obtain.

The formation of ridges varies from roofing material to material. In stone slab they are usually formed of cut stone ridge pieces although they are occasionally of lead set on a timber roll. In plain and pantile they are formed from half-round tiles with, in the case of pantile, small pieces of tile inserted to fill the intra tile gaps—galletting. Ridges in slate roofs can be of stone, lead or even of tile though this latter is less attractive. It is important to be careful in selecting the ridge members; red clay ridge tiles can be very obtrusive when used with a slate finish. One traditional form, still occasionally seen in the country, is the ridge of 'wrestler' slates. Slates, like all roof coverings, are a fundamental part of the vernacular of an area; the architecture of the Lake District is based upon the practical and sensible use of slate to form drip strings over windows and doors, porches and canopies, for the vertical facing of exposed timber lintols and for the chimney caps.

Left: The traditional stone slabs of upland houses. Problems arise from erosion of the undersides and 'slip' due to the failure of the pegging. This is a very heavy roof and places a great load on the roof structure

Below left: Traditional clay pantile is distinctive in colour, weathers well and is set to a high pitch. There are no acceptable substitutes and even pantile set at a low pitch can look poor

Below right: Slates were common in the 19th and early 20th centuries, and are today much undervalued

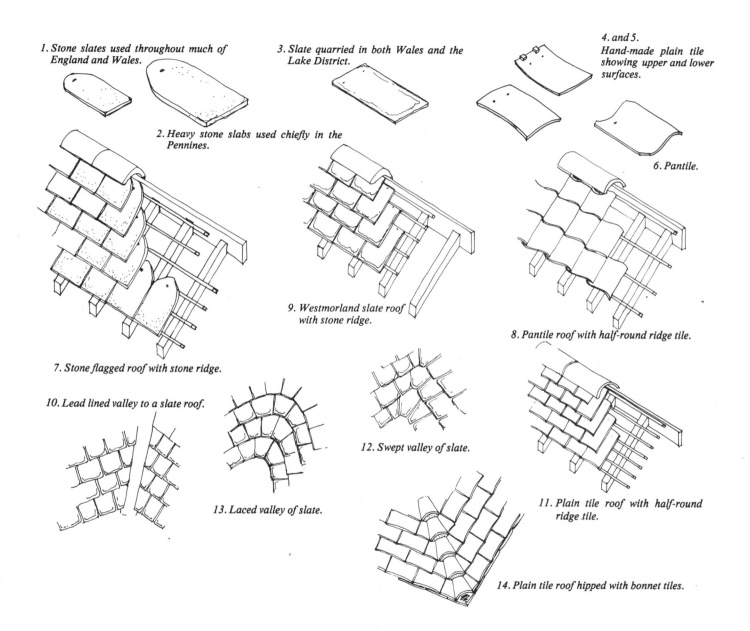

1. Stone slates used throughout much of England and Wales.

3. Slate quarried in both Wales and the Lake District.

4. and 5. Hand-made plain tile showing upper and lower surfaces.

2. Heavy stone slabs used chiefly in the Pennines.

6. Pantile.

9. Westmorland slate roof with stone ridge.

8. Pantile roof with half-round ridge tile.

7. Stone flagged roof with stone ridge.

10. Lead lined valley to a slate roof.

12. Swept valley of slate.

13. Laced valley of slate.

11. Plain tile roof with half-round ridge tile.

14. Plain tile roof hipped with bonnet tiles.

DOORS DOORWAYS AND PORCHES

The form of doorways and the degree of decoration which they incorporated depended upon the building material employed and the status of the house or its occupant. The doorway was a feature which lent itself to emphasis and elaboration and hence it became, and indeed still is, the subject of many of the owners aspirations, ambitions and pretensions.

Medieval doorways are comparatively rare. However the great spate of building which took place after the accession of James I is evident in the number of inscribed and ornamented doorways which still exist. Often the doorway of this time was retained and incorporated into a later rebuilding. These early seventeenth-century doors were often a crude version of the Tudor flat arch—false four centred—with splayed jambs and arch lintol and the whole surmounted by a drip or label mould with dropped and returned ends. Gradually through the century these were replaced by a simpler opening of plain or splayed jambs and lintol, but with the lintol elaborately decorated with a variety of patterns and mouldings. These generally included the date of construction of the house and the initials of the owners. The arrangement of these, for example, either T B M, or T B M (Thomas and Margaret Braithwaite) provides valuable information on the building and the circumstances of its construction. The doors themselves were originally of oak or elm, either simple braced and battened doors or with the centre battens recessed and with planted mouldings over. Early doors were heavy and were hung from brackets in the stone or brick jamb with a simple crossbolt. Later they were hinged to an inner door frame and equipped with hinges, locks, etc.

Two-panel doors, with raised or fielded panels appear from the latter years of the seventeenth century, often with a planted moulded centre rail and or a skirting. These are sometimes found in older properties relegated to the back premises and are well worth retaining and re-using if at all possible. Usually they incorporate 'L' hinges and good iron furniture handmade by the local smith.

The commonest Georgian door in use throughout the eighteenth century was the six-panel door again with fielded or raised panels. When these were used externally they usually included a geometric pattern fanlight over them. Almost always these were executed in pine or deal and painted, only in larger houses were doors, and particularly internal doors, of mahogany or other hardwood.

The doorcases of the grander Georgian houses changed as the changing fashions of eighteenth-century architecture itself changed; from the simplified baroque—rusticated jambs, heavy entablature and cornice, emphasised keystone and triangular, segmental, scroll broken pediment, to the refinements and low relief of the later neo-classical architecture of the Adam Brothers and James Wyatt.

During the century the planted bolection moulds which appeared in early work, both in the joinery and the case gave way to moulds run in the actual framing of the door itself. The fashions expressed in the decoration of doors and doorcases in the grander houses were adapted for quite modest houses in simplified and cruder form.

A further emphasis to the principal door was the construction of a small portico or porch, complete with columns, usually of the Tuscan Roman Doric or Ionic order complete with frieze, entablature and cornice. The introduction of the Greek style with its fluted Doric columns into domestic architecture in the 1830's and the survival of this style in the North until the early 1880's saw classical doorcases and porches used as a general feature of villas and terrace houses as well as larger mansions.

The widespread use of the six-panelled door lasted over one hundred and fifty years and was gradually replaced by the adaptation of these to four, six and even eight panels, each with long narrow panels. The panels were bordered by planted mouldings, sometimes of Greek derivation and later with more robust bolection moulds, occasionally with round or arched-headed panels.

The variety obtainable within the framework of the six-panelled door was immense and many regional and area variations and fashions were developed. For external doors the lower two panels were set flush with the frame; the lower panels were replaced by a single panel or a patterned panel

1. *16th- and 17th-century ledged and panelled door usually in oak*
2. *17th- and early 18th-century two-panelled door with wide centre rail, occasionally with applied moulding. The fielded panels are usually flush on one face*
3. *18th-century six-panelled door; early examples have fielded panels, later the panels were flat with superimposed mouldings. Lower panels were sometimes set flush*
4. *Victorian six- or four-panelled doors with a variety of ornament*
5. *Popular 15 light glazed—French—door of today*
6. *Rogue fashion—now even Art Deco—the 'rising sun' door*

of 'X' or other form; the small upper panels were glazed; the panels were either plain, or fielded or included small bead mouldings set on to the panel face. The range and type of door furniture often gives an indication of the age of the door; 'L' shaped hinges continued to be used on doors for much of the eighteenth century; escutcheons, locks and bolts themselves were all hand forged, the product of the local smith. Brass furniture, knobs, knockers, locks, etc., changed in design alongside the change in fashion and design of the doors themselves; some items like knockers grew to have particular association—the double 'S' scroll knocker of the Doctor, various urns, swags, Medusa heads and rings were common. All of these have now been worn to a smooth finish by decades of loving polishing or have too often been overpainted. There is really no substitute for the continual polishing of brass, laquer eventually dulls and discolours. If the effort of continual cleaning is too much, many of the designs are and were also produced in cast iron which can be painted or blacked.

The use of the shine of brass on and around doorways, like the buttons on a military tunic, has lasted. Even the Victorians added to the tradition by the use of brass-covered outer steps, still found occasionally.

With the eventual fall from fashion of the classical door, based on the Georgian six panel precedent, Victorian doors proper assumed many forms. Executed in hardwoods or pitch pine—the striated timber normally associated with the pews of non-conformist churches—outer doors were generally glazed with a geometric pattern of coloured glasses or single or twin panels of etched and cut glass. Many of these panels have gone; either they were out of fashion—regarded as too old fashioned, or they were broken and costly to replace. Where they survive every attempt should be made to keep or replace them as an integral part of the Victorian house. There are still specialist glass firms who can do this work.

The coming of the Arts and Crafts Movement towards the end of the nineteenth century had a profound and lasting effect upon the design of the English house both inside and out. Architects and designers like William Morris, Phillip Webb, C. F. A. Voysey, Baillie Scott, C. R. Ashbee, and Ernest Gimson dismissed the pretentions from domestic design to return it closer to the vernacular base from which it sprang. The architecture, if that is what it is, of suburbia

Simple modern oak door in a 17th-century opening
Above: Simple country doors, one with two glazed upper panels
Below: Early battened door in hooded doorcase. Note the primitive 'light'
over. A simple door appropriate to a simple setting

18th- and 19th-century doors and doorcases in variety, from wide country doors to narrow town doors. The Ionic porch shows the Greek influence strong in the North

with its emphasis on individual likes, tastes and whims is particularly English. Not the least important element in the houses which grew up to surround most of our main towns during the period, are the entrances and doors. A curious and familiar mixture of Arts and Crafts and jokey Art Deco. Nooksy half-timbered portals, doors with circular and elliptical glazed panels showing ships, trees and never-never-land cottages, others with the rising sun emblazoned in glass or heart-shaped openings are to be seen in any walk around suburbia.

The more serious attempts at a folk art style harked back to the traditional ledged braced and battened doors in untreated or fumed oak, with, on the better buildings, hand wrought hinges and door furniture. Decoration of iron studs with hinges exposed on the outer face of external doors was popular.

The glazed door, or French door, is really a mark of the twenties, though there are older examples. No polite upper-class play of the period was complete without a French door-window in its set through which the hero/heroine or villain could make his or her unannounced entrance. With the development of interest in the flower garden during this century they are both useful and pleasant and have hence remained in favour. Bar-divided glazed doors in either timber or metal are common place.

The most important recent change in door design came with the introduction of the flush door, first seen in the twenties and with its figured veneering, a mark of the thirties. The flush door was and is available in all finishes and types to suit all purposes. They attracted the housewife in that they were easy to clean and keep clean, and her husband in that they were plain and simple and above all were fashionable and cheap. Today they are available in every veneer, hardwood or plastic finish imaginable and are eminently useful. However, they should be used with great care in incorporating them into old houses and cottages. Used carefully they can be a useful plain ploy to a highly-ornate surround, or to show clearly which parts of a building are new and of today. Modern doors made solely of glass can be used most successfully in old surrounds and settings where no model exists for the door as it would have been, or to highlight attention to the surround or to create a visual flow of space from room to room, though they are expensive.

WINDOWS

Like doors and doorways, the earliest examples of window openings and glazing generally encountered, date from the first years of the seventeenth century. These openings were simple rectangular 'lights', set within chamfered stone jambs, cill and lintol, often linked in groups; the joining vertical stone members being the mullions. These windows, again like the doors, were often surmounted by a label or drip mould with drop ends and returns. The possibilities of grouping these single lights to form larger windows extended not only in a horizontal direction—linked by mullions—but also vertically, in which case the jointing members were called transoms. More important houses had moulded jambs and lintols, though usually the cills were left either plain or simply chamfered. Rare examples survive of oak window frames of this period in isolated areas like the Lake District. The glazing was either direct into the stone surround to form a fixed light, or was set into a metal frame capable of opening. The glazing of small quarries—regularly shaped pieces of glass—in lead was usual, strengthened by a vertical iron rod set into the cill and lintol to which the glazing was wired.

Early glass, being handmade is often greenish in colour, of varying thickness and with bubbles and other marks. In the glazing of many older windows in the nineteenth century, the Victorians exploited the sparkle of this type of glazing derived from the variations in the glass and reset the glass at various angles and planes. An extreme example is to be seen at Haddon Hall, Derbyshire.

Wrought iron window fittings of this period can be very decorative; hinges and casement stays with twisted shafts and scrolled and tapered ends.

The introduction to England of the sash window, an integral element of post-Renaissance architecture was quickly followed by its general adoption except in remote areas and the uplands. The vertical sash was used for almost all new building and for the replacement of the earlier Carolean '+' pattern of moulded mullion and transom. At first it was of twelve or twenty-four lights, with thick moulded glazing bars and with the boxed frame which contained the sash weights set close to the outer face of the brickwork or masonry. Often there was no cill as such other than a lead flashing beneath the wood cill. These windows were then exemplified by the proportion of joinery to glass and the wide outer frame around the window. As the eighteenth century progressed so too did the design of the sash window. Glazing bars were refined to the narrowest of sections, the panes of glass were standardised in proportion—based generally upon the classical 'Golden section', the number of panes generally of three wide and four deep—six to each sash—and the sash boxes set well back from the face of the building partly hidden in a structural reveal. With some experience it is possible to date appoximately a sash window depending upon these factors.

To improve daylighting standards, sashes were sometimes grouped together, either side by side, or in groups of one central sash flanked by two narrow fixed sashes—a common treatment and one which can be useful in improving daylighting standards in older buildings where the retention of the sash is important.

The horizontal sliding sash or Yorkshire Light was a common 'cottage' window of the eighteenth and nineteenth centuries. The sash slides in grooves at cill and at head, a form appropriate to square window opening. Problems occur in that the sashes often stick. Casements were however also common in humbler homes and often only one single pane of a fixed bar-divided window would form a tiny casement.

Fashionable forms of window were 'translated' into the vernacular; Venetian or Palladian windows (a single round-headed sash flanked by two narrow sashes with square heads at the spring line of the semi-circular top) were not uncommon and elaborate round-headed traceried windows, either in the Gothick or geometric manner were used for staircases.

The methods of manufacture of glass dictated the scale and patterns of glazing up to the nineteenth century when the benefits of new technology enabled sheets of large size to be made. The earliest glazed windows used very small diamond shaped or rectangular quarries of glass, held together in lead cames. Even the size of the Georgian bar-divided window pane was dictated by the maximum prac-

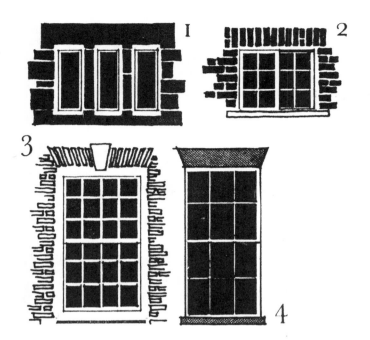

1. *16th- and 17th-century single casements in stone jambs, transoms and mullions*
2. *Horizontal sliding sash or Yorkshire Light*
3. *Early Georgian 24 light sash with exposed sash boxes and thick glazing bars*
4. *Later Georgian 12 light sash—the glazing bars refined*

element. The rectangular panes produced by this method are called 'crown' glass, because of the crown of thickness and the spin markings within the pane. Where such remains it should be carefully protected during building work and preserved, it is almost impossible to replace.

The great beauty of crown glass comes not only from its irregularities and markings, it often contains air bubbles and spin marks, but the changes in the thickness and the levels of the surface create, with changing light, life and sparkle within the overall window.

Genuine 'bulls eyes' show clearly the point where the rod has broken away and the sharp rim of this break. However, the insatiable desire to incorporate these curiosities in new work has resulted in a variety of reproductions and substitutes. Some are merely pressed, either in glass or plastic, or where they are still produced by traditional techniques, they are now valued for the 'bulls eye' alone.

The change in manufacturing techniques and the production of cheap glass by sheet drawing, enabled panes to be greatly increased in size during the nineteenth century. Small barred divisions were abandoned in almost all houses except

ticable size to which glass could be made. Glass was, until the advent of the sheet-drawing techniques, cast or spun. Spun glass was the commonest method in general use and for this a rod was dipped into the molten glass metal by the glass maker and then hand spun until the knob had flattened and expanded by centrifugal force to a disc; a disc thinnest at the outer edges and thickest at the central point. This disc was cooled and broken from the rod. Rectangular pieces of glass, to form panes were then cut from the disc, the remainder including the central knop going·to waste. This central knop or 'bulls eye' was used for unimportant glazing, rear windows, the windows of stores and humbler homes, and only in the present century became regarded as a decorative

717,—" Flashing-out " Crown glass.

Single casements grouped in various ways with plain or moulded jambs and mullions, some with and others without label mouldings. Earliest examples have round or arch headed lights

EIGHTEENTH-
AND EARLY NINETEENTH-
CENTURY WINDOWS

Earliest windows show the wide band of the sash boxes. Later these were placed in reveals. Glazing bars, thick at first—top left—were refined through the century—top right. To permit larger glazed areas, sashes were grouped with fixed narrow lights. The Victorians used a variety of glazing patterns—right

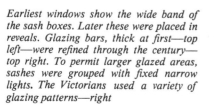

for rural buildings and humbler homes in favour of the large two-paned sashes, although at first this arrangement was approached gradually, six panes, then four and finally two. The change in the facade of the house was considerable. No longer was the window a complex pattern of small panes, but now appeared as two sizeable blank holes punched in the facade at each window opening. The great house of Chatsworth in Derbyshire was changed considerably when new large pane glazing was introduced in the nineteenth century as a fashionable replacement of the older bar-divided sashes. There the glass was polished plate with bevelled edges.

The Arts and Crafts movement and the Queen Anne revival of the last years of the nineteenth century saw a return to older patterns with bar divisions. The growth of suburbia before and after the First World War enabled this revival to flourish, even to providing leaded glazing to casements and elaborate-coloured glazed pictures, often used in the upper panes of bays and windows. Metal window frames were and are available either as plain casements or bar divided. The horizontal panes favoured between the Wars, and typical of the domestic building of the thirties are usually associated with emerging 'modernism'.

Now the range of windows available for use is wider than ever. Casements in timber or metal, with or without hopper hung panes; sashes in timber or aluminium; centre pivoted timber windows or with large panes associated with long narrow hopper openings. The metal can be pretreated or galvanised and the timber can be hardwood or softwood, to be painted, stained or plastic covered. In approaching new work associated with older buildings or the restoration and improvement of these, care and judgement should be applied to the choice of suitable alternatives.

Bay windows have a historic pedigree. They appear in the planning of the medieval Manor House—to light the dais end of the Great Hall, they are an important feature of the houses of the early Renaissance, often carried through several stories, and although they were not a feature of the great houses of eighteenth century, they survived in medium sized and smaller dwellings—Rectories, farmhouses, and cottages, usually to provide better lighting and extra space to the principal living rooms but rarely extending through more than one storey. The detailing of these windows changed along with the changes in more general windows, at first

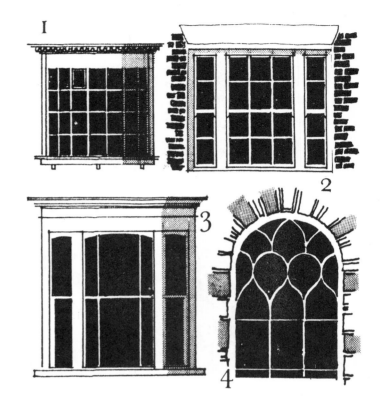

1. Traditional 'shop' bow window—often with one or two opening panes. Grander examples have sashes. The weight of the entablature — the vertical piece between the window proper and the cornice is omitted from most mass-produced replicas

2. Grouped sashes — 18th and 19th centuries

3. Mid 19th-century Bay windows.

4. Decorative staircase window head—Teesdale early 19th century.

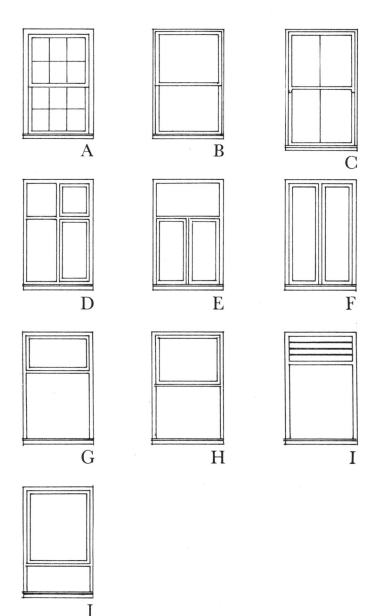

A

B

C

D

E

F

G

H

I

J

casements, set in stone frames, then sashes in a timber window case. They have always been popular. Bay windows became a status symbol applied to almost any dwelling above the meanest standard and are a hallmark of the Victorian and Edwardian terrace house with bays at either ground or first floor level or both.

Large semi-circular bays were prominent features in suburban house design in the inter-war period, and bays in general enjoyed a popularity at that time which was partially eclipsed in the post-war rebuilding, the creation of new housing estates and new towns. They survive today, more or less as bay windows in new development and in the reactionary search for humanity and character in the present vogue for Bow windows.

Bow windows were almost always 'shop' windows in either town or village. Simple bows had casement openings or in the humbler examples single-pane openings. Grander and later examples had a series of sashes linked by wide mullions. They were invariably surmounted by a plain classical frieze, entablature and cornice with either a lead flat roof or occasionally a small pitched roof over them. Bow windows so dressed in their classical garb can be very attractive windows and elegant elements in a design. However, they have become popular, though their various associations, to universal use irrespective of the sense or appropriateness of the situation. The present day bow window, selected off the manufacturer's peg, fitted without much thought and a lot of sentiment, sans entablature, cornice and almost everything, capped with roofing felt appears ludicrous. The lesson is to use them with extreme care, and if in any doubt as to their suitability don't.

WINDOW TYPES IN PRESENT DAY USE

A, B and C
Sash windows, bar divided, single paned and with centre bars

D, E and F
Casement varieties in the same type of opening

G and H
Hoppers and I with louvres

J centre pivoted light

D, E and F are clumsy alternatives—H, I and J are better modern arrangements

Right: New windows can be inserted into existing openings where the cost of exact replacement cannot be justified—an acceptable solution in a terrace of 19th-century artisans cottages in County Durham where the whole group has been treated together

Opposite page: Much of the character of a house depends on the grouping of windows and the relation of window to wall. This can be easily destroyed by inserting new windows of different area and proportion

COLOUR
AND DECORATION

The most important colours and combinations of colours in any house or cottage are those of the basic materials of construction; stone, brick, rendering, clay tile, stone slab, slate, etc. Most of these, having a pervious natural finish, are affected by wind and weather. In towns and cities they blacken with soot, though this is nowadays much improved through the adoption of the principle of cleaner air; in the countryside they mellow with lichens, mosses and the patina of age that weather and, to a certain extent, decay brings. Pleasing decay—that indefinable stage at which a building has matured and weathered yet not suffered material deterioration is a beautiful state to behold but difficult to hold for any length of time. If the brickwork, masonry or any other element is badly discoloured, then consideration might be given to cleaning this. Layers of dirt hide not only good materials but also water and they help form injurious salts which may help to break down the surface.

Only surface dirt should be removed so that the wall will still, if the cleaning has been carried out carefully, retain some of the underneath weathering. It is not really the aim of cleaning to present a totally scrubbed and primmed building looking brand new. Cleaning should be carried out by experienced workmen and by the gentlest possible means. The only absolutely safe method is to spray with water and remove the dirt with stiff-bristle brushes, making sure that no water penetrates through open joints to the interior. It is advisable to inspect and point if necessary prior to washing in this way. A wooden scraper may be used and the specialised technique of steam cleaning, though this is more expensive. Each building to be cleaned must be judged according to the materials of construction, their state of repair and condition and the amount of dirt to be removed. Drastic methods such as sand blasting, bush hammering or the use of rotary grinders and discs may all be used in certain conditions, but they give a new 'look' to the building and remove not only the dirt but a good proportion of the surface of the building as well.

Cleaning is only one aspect of good maintenance. An essential preliminary is to check rainwater disposal, flashings, gutters and downpipes. Proper pointing is necessary and it is important not to use materials such as rich cement which may shrink or crack or be less porous than the basic materials themselves. Silicone treatment after cleaning reduces the porosity of the surface forming a barrier against the penetration of water and helping it to run away. The same barrier can however check the outward movement from the stone or brick into the air and cause surface break-up.

Washing the stone or brick fabric with lime is traditional to many areas including the Lake District, and parts of North Yorkshire and County Durham. Over many years, this layer, usually replaced every three or four years, builds up to a thick skin. Limewash itself attracts and holds moisture; lime-washed buildings appear grey and lifeless on wet days. To overcome this and to prevent the lime washing off with heavy rain a binding agent is often mixed in—traditionally this was tallow or skimmed milk though nowadays more modern agents are used. Lime has, however, a soft yet shining quality not associated with modern exterior paints and the thickening of the skin of lime softens the contours of a rough stone building.

There are now many alternatives available including external emulsions, and textured paints with nylon, ground stone dust and other additives. These have the great benefits that they are weather impervious, do not need the regular replacement of lime and can give a variety of colours other than white. Before applying any of these finishes be sure that the existing surface will not break down after application and that a bond between the two finishes is possible. Be wary of painting over natural materials not already painted such as brick and stone; once applied to these materials, it is difficult though not impossible to remove. If these materials are dirty and disfigured it is probably better to clean them than to overpaint.

In choosing any colour for colourwashing or painting a building remember that the colour will be seen in large areas, and that it is a wise precaution to try a panel out first before finally deciding. Also remember the other colours which are basic to the building and cannot be changed yet will be seen alongside the new colour—the roof, other natural materials such as brick walls, stone dressings and even climbing plants. The safest but perhaps the most timid solution is to aim for soft pastel colours which nearly resemble the natural materials themselves—stone, beige, mushroom, pale greens and yellows, etc. Large areas of violent and assertive colour, deep purples, acid yellows and emerald greens can easily overpower any building although dark colours, deep browns and sage greens for example can be highly effective. It all really depends on how the colour is to be used—what the other associated colours are to be, how the overall scheme is to be handled, what the setting of the building is—whether an isolated country dwelling or a town house within a street and whether the architecture of the building can take such colour dominance. A simple artisans cottage with minimum areas of other colour and simple detailing will not generally respond to such treatment whereas a grander town house, with large areas of window and door case, an elaborate porch and large crowning cornice might suit a bold scheme admirably.

Some colours are notoriously difficult to select and handle, pinks for instance. They can be very strident and just too pink or they can be very soft and little more than a coloured haze. Warm colours are usually more amenable to old buildings and nothing looks better in some circumstances than a soft warm pink wash. Provided that the colourwashing doesn't begin to look too untidy, let the colour soften with age and fading, sometimes really beautiful effects can be produced; the ochre washes used for instance on north Italian villas look their best when gently weathered and faded. Remember always that a colour looks considerably stronger when it has been applied to the large areas of a building's exterior.

Colourwashing can suffer where the walls meet the ground surface through the rebounding splashing of rain especially where the wall surfaces meet open ground or flower beds. A traditional technique was to stop the rendering above the ground line, generally on to a wooden lath and with an outward curve in the render. The surface between ground level and this render stop line was then painted with pitch or some other black finish. This is known in some areas as

Colour and tone can effect dramatic changes. 1, the basic stone house, 2, black and white in the Cumbrian tradition and 3, a deep colour with the sparkle of white

BAYS AND BOWS

Bay windows can assume many shapes and forms; some old and modern examples

Modern window insertions can make or mar the building
Left: New cottage windows emphasise with deep reveals the basic shape and proportions of the facade
Below: New off-the-peg windows of different shapes have materially altered this old farmhouse

43

'boot topping' and prevents soil, and other dirt being splashed back on to the coloured finish.

The selection of a wash colour for the major wall surfaces is an important part in the preparation of the overall colour scheme. The other important selections are those for the exposed joinery elements; windows and door frames, cornices, gutters, rainwater pipes, exposed plumbing and doors. Generally, plumbing items are anything but beautiful unless they are of lead in which case the hopper heads, the cast pipes and the lugs should be carefully cleaned and restored. Plumbing items should therefore be painted 'out' as far as possible if these are of cast iron and if of plastic, a suitable colour, which melts into the background, chosen. Stone colours and light browns for stone buildings, light and medium browns for brick structures and a suitable colour, perhaps slightly darker than the main colour, for those buildings colourwashed.

The easiest solution for window frames, doorcases and cornices is to paint them white, which mixes satisfactorily with almost any background colour and where dark colours are used can give sparkle and vibrancy to the scheme. Nevertheless a colour scheme is a personal statement not only of the buildings intrinsic character but of the owners taste, imagination and sensitivity and hence white windows, etc., are not an invariable rule for a good scheme. The Cumbrian tradition of black windows and doorcases combined with whitewashing is most satisfactory. If, however, you are in any doubt—use white. White itself can vary greatly. Try to avoid the whitest of whites—the titanium-based (brilliant) paints which can be too white and somewhat insensitive in an old building.

Cornices and gutters provide a visual stop to a building and separate visually the roof and walls and should be clearly shown and even accentuated by the choice of colour. In some areas, for example in and around Stokesley, North Yorkshire, there is a tradition of enormous elaborate cornices, complete with dentils and pendants. These demand careful consideration and choice of colour in order for them to play their proper visual role to top the high brick facades.

Doors, being relatively small patches of colour in the total scheme can be treated with a little more bravado, though again appropriateness to the situation of the building and its

Eighteenth-century artisans cottages—Castle Eden, County Durham.

surroundings must be considered; whether the scheme can take the jauntiness of a bright colour or whether the whole character of the place is muted and sedate. Certainly bright, even strident colours can look well and most effective for example on town doors where there is plenty of white or other neutral surround to separate the basic material of the accompanying walls or their colourwash. It is a good precept to isolate the colour of a door by a surround and doorcase of white. Piling colour upon colour, door with doorcase with walls and window frames, etc., can easily promote visual indigestion. As to the colours themselves, basic black or white can be most stimulating especially when graced by polished brass as can many of the primary colours—reds, yellows, blues provided these are not too acid and have an inherent sparkle. This is really a field where the flair of the designer pays handsomely. If in doubt keep on trying, after all a door or doors are easily retrieved elements in a colour scheme.

Doorcases and fanlights are generally best painted white especially where the fanlight pattern is intricate and interesting except of course where the walls surrounding the cases are washed white. Doors with fielded panels are best treated as a whole, although some later Victorian and Edwardian doors which have attractive mouldings can be picked out in other colours or white. The safest, but by no means always the most interesting schemes are those based on a harmony of colours. If the doorcase itself has interesting mouldings or patterns, then these too can be picked out. Be most careful in using gilding; it can be totally appropriate and decorative to a door of scale and importance in a house of grandeur but looks out of place in a cottage and the like. Gold paint tarnishes rapidly externally to a dirty black. If gilding is used then it is worth while using gold leaf.

45

The tradition of limewash, strong in parts of North Yorkshire, Durham and the Lake District. Cottage at Langton, County Durham

Unity of decoration without the loss of individuality brings great benefits to the terrace. Grange Crescent, Sunderland, Tyne and Wear

AROUND AND ABOUT

The setting of the house or cottage creates the character of the group and complements the architecture and treatment of the building. Like all the things which we can do to buildings our treatment of it can make or mar. Too many good houses have been spoiled by the treatment of their settings; the choice of gates, railings and fences, light fittings, walls and boundaries, paths and drives, paved terraces and even planting and gardens. All these and other items in the buildings setting should be in scale and character with the building, its size and pretentions, its importance and its materials and decoration. Avoid the brash and phoney; if the building is of good stone with a stone roof then do not introduce multicoloured concrete paviors to form a path or approach—find an alternative natural material; if the building is of old brick, then do not introduce reconstructed stone with concrete dressings for a boundary wall—stick to brick. All this sounds very basic advice, but time after time inconsequentialities and disasters occur.

Brick or stone paving for paths can be assembled in a multiplicity of patterns and arrangements without recourse to non-natural materials or a coating of tarmacadam, but try always to aim for regular patterns as against the much admired crazy paving. For drives and approach roads consider using gravel which can now be top dressed to prevent weed growth and is both cheap and attractive.

Gates reflect the importance of the house just as much as the entrance door. Fine stone or brick gate piers should be treasured and preserved, and a gate to complement them inserted. Nothing looks better than a timber gate, of solid proportion—even perhaps using one of the elegant Edwardian patterns with an upper panel of turned bars. Painted white and set in fine piers they look exceedingly handsome. If you choose to use the more expensive wrought iron, then make sure it is wrought iron proper and not bent and welded thin steel bar. There are so many so-called wrought iron gates on the market, mass-produced which in-situ look much too light and flimsy. It is still possible to find wrought iron craftsmen in our towns and villages, though their work, rightly, is far from cheap.

Gates then should be appropriate to the house, a simple wooden gate for a cottage; a grander wooden gate or an iron gate for a more substantial house and so on. For wide, drive

The tradition of white walls and greys or black to emphasise openings. Knock village, Cumbria

The simplicity of white, cottage door at Hurworth, County Durham

MATERIALS AND COLOUR

Above left: Traditional materials weather gracefully into the landscape, farmhouse near Crakehall, North Yorkshire
Above right: Simple rules on the uniformity of materials can be success-fully broken, Church at Sustead, Norfolk
Left: Even materials like corrugated iron can weather happily into the landscape, Great Bavington, Northumberland

*Above left and below   : Roof colours are very important, especially the
rich reds of clay pantile. North Yorkshire*
*Above right: The warmth of old brickwork should be protected and treated
with great care*

51

or roadway gates in a rural situation why not an agricultural gate or a traditional five-bar gate with hinges and swing catch to match.

Fashion certainly goes in circles of time, the present vogue for old city gas light fittings either wall mounted on brackets or mounted on a cast iron pole uses elements long discarded by the city lighting authorities. They are really urban components and set in the surroundings of a rural dwelling can look oddly out of place. The vogue for the trappings of the horse-drawn carriage age—carriage lamps, wheels used as decorative objects in themselves or incorporated into fences and gates—still persists and can be regarded as part of the 'stage setting' of the cottage. There are however elegantly designed, simple modern light fittings, both standards and wall mounted, which because of their simplicity and shape fit into almost any renovation scheme. The plain glass or break-proof spun plastic globes set on a black metal arm or base are some of the best.

Almost all cast iron railing was removed from the boundaries of terrace houses in our towns and cities during the last war. Decorative cast iron only survives in occasional stretches of railing and for such features as balconies, porches, finials to roofs, light fittings and pavement manhole covers, etc., The result has been a patchwork of replacements—hedges, brick walls, timber fences of every type, concrete block walls and metal fences usually of welded steel bar. Cast iron is now expensive to replace, but in considering a renovation scheme for a terrace house try to co-operate with neighbours, not only as far as decoration is concerned, but in such matters as fencing, gates, etc., The scheme illustrated on page 47 was completed by erecting a simple metal railing and gates throughout the whole terrace.

Garden design is a very personal expression of interest and enthusiasm which nevertheless should be related to the building, the paths and approaches and boundary walls. A formal house demands a formal garden whether this is a complicated affair or simple lawn; a rural cottage, attuned to a cottage garden of a riotous mixture of vegetables and flowers can suffer if transformed with a formal setting of regular flower beds and parksified bedding. If there are good trees around seek to keep them; if they darken the house, see what can be done by careful and judicious pruning rather than felling. If they are old and dangerous get expert advice on what needs to be removed, which limbs are liable to fall and what other tree surgery can be done. Once felled they cannot be replaced in anything like their mature glory. When choosing new trees and larger shrubs for planting think what they will look like throughout the year; the flowering cherries are beautiful, but for only a very short period, most native forest trees look well throughout the year and change with the changing seasons.

Hedges are a pleasant alternative to fences and railings but they need constant attention to feed and to keep in trim. Cypress hedges are suited to formal gardens and have a beautiful texture; privet is a dirt-collecting shrub redolent of our industrial towns; beech is highly attractive but slow to establish and grow. More use might be made of quickthorn or even of shrub roses. Roses make a most effective barbed-wire fence to keep out or in dogs and children.

The surroundings of buildings are as important as the buildings them-selves. Street improvement at Exeter, Devon

EXTERNAL COLOUR

Above left and left: Elm Hill, Norwich
Above centre: Early 19th-century town house, Old Elvet, Durham
Above right: Country pinkwash, near Durham.

Opposite page
Above left: Market Harborough, Leicestershire
Above centre: 18th-century porch, Bow Lane, Durham
Above right: Sophisticated architecture needs sophisticated colour. Doorway, Old Elvet, Durham.
Below left: Attractive late 18th-century 'twin' doors, Durham
Below centre: Muted colours for a town cottage door, Durham
Below right: Bold colour door in a bold early 18th-century doorcase, Durham

Cottage conversion at Romaldkirk, County Durham with new entrance forecourt. Above: Before and Below: After

Conversion and extension scheme at Eden's Cottage, Heslington, York. A new forecourt retaining trees. Architects: York University Design Unit. Above: Before and Below: After

AROUND AND ABOUT

Many houses border open spaces like the traditional village green—above at Stokesley, North Yorkshire, or the hard surfaced square—below at Blanchland, Northumberland

Cottage at Cracoe, North Yorkshire.

Architects: Wales, Wales and Rawson, Skipton, North Yorkshire

Barn conversion at Little Walwick, Northumberland. Above: Before and Below: After completion
Architects: Douglass Wise and Partners, Newcastle upon Tyne

Above: Little Walwick House, Northumberland
Right: Above and Below: Shandy Hall, Coxwold, North Yorkshire, before and after restoration
Architects: Leckenby, Keighley and Groom, York

OLD HOUSES TO NEW HOMES

So far this book has tried to cover the various aspects and features of the houses and cottages one would expect to encounter in looking at buildings for conversion and improvement. It has also tried to set down something of the traditional—vernacular—methods and techniques of building in order that we may know a little about the buildings we are likely to be dealing with. As was said in the introduction, too many conversions and improvements of recent years have been destructive to the quality and character of the cottage and house. Many happily have not. This section of the book now looks at some of those recently-executed schemes which have not only created a new home but have retained and in some cases enhanced the original character.

First, the improvement and extension of existing cottages and houses, to make them suitable for present day standards and requirements for living or to extend and enlarge them. The factors most commonly met with in old buildings and which are unacceptable by today's standards are: poor day-lighting standards—small windows; primitive servicing—ramshackle or inadequate bathrooms and kitchens and basic structural problems—shifting walls, leaking gutters and roofs, brick and masonry decay and the associated problems of rot and worm activity, decaying timbers and joinery, dangerous electrical wiring and rising damp. In rural situations these problems are aggravated by the addition of the problems of inadequate private water supplies, poor or non existent sewage disposal—septic tanks, and the task ahead can be daunting and expensive. To convert and improve a house or cottage well is not cheap. Grant aid can help but may not invariably be forthcoming.

In many cases the house or cottage has probably been the property of old people or of a landlord, and whilst the services may have been satisfactory for them, funds have not always been available for large-scale overhaul. Probably the best advice is to find an architect or sound builder who will know what needs to be done and what this will cost. Remember that whilst new building work and some restoration is not VAT rateable, repair work is. Finding an architect is not as easy as it may seem. The services you require from him are detailed and very time consuming. A small local practice is often the best target, but find out what else he or she has done in the area, look at it and see if this is what you want. Local offices of the Royal Institute of British Architects can provide help and advice.

The fees charged by registered architects are related to the size and cost of the work and are a percentage of this. The fee, therefore, is somewhat difficult to establish accurately particularly in dealing with old properties where the unexpected is almost invariably the rule. The Professional Institute (the RIBA) sets down a minimum scale of fees for what is called 'normal service'. For work to an existing building this is 13 per cent for work costing up to £2,500 and $12\frac{1}{2}$ per cent for work costing between £2,500 and £8,000. A scale of fees (minimum) is set down for 'partial service' and these should be discussed with the architect. Normal service includes—preparation of plans and drawings, their submission for the necessary Planning and Bye Law approvals to the Local Authority, preparing specifications or other matter for obtaining tenders for the work, preparing a contract, advising on the selection of a builder or other specialists required, preparing a timetable, supervising the work and issuing certificates for the payment of the builder and in general seeing the work right through. These fees do not include travelling and other expenses, the cost of prints, etc., which can, because of the numbers of copies required, be rather high, and other special work. These are covered by a separate non-percentage charge. Charges by Surveyors are the same. Fees charged by others, who are not members of the professional bodies are not controlled and may be arrived at by negotiation. However, unless the work is of a very minor nature the safest course is through an architect. In every case you will require someone, unless you are able to do this for yourself, to survey the building and prepare drawings of the work proposed for the necessary legal submissions and for grant applications.

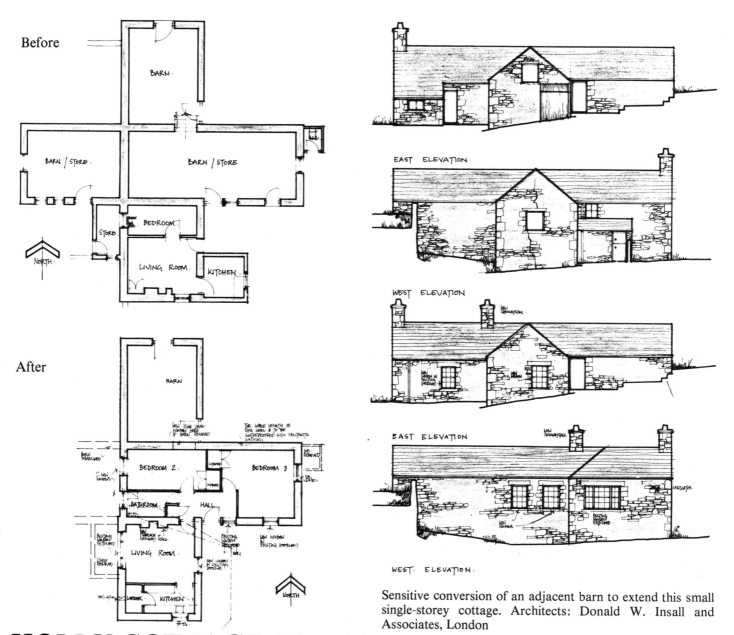

Before

BARN

BARN / STORE

BARN / STORE

NORTH

STORE

BEDROOM

LIVING ROOM

KITCHEN

After

BARN

BEDROOM 2

BEDROOM 3

BATHROOM

HALL

LIVING ROOM

LARDER

KITCHEN

NORTH

EAST ELEVATION

WEST ELEVATION

EAST ELEVATION

WEST ELEVATION

Sensitive conversion of an adjacent barn to extend this small single-storey cottage. Architects: Donald W. Insall and Associates, London

HOLLY COTTAGE, Blanchland, Northumberland

Holly Cottage, Blanchland, Northumberland after completion

UPPER CHURCH STREET, SPENNYMOOR,
County Durham

Improvement scheme for a row of colliery houses. Above: Before and Below: After.
Architects: Sedgefield District Council

This row of colliery cottages was built in 1870, and although the fabric was sound they lacked many of the basic amenities. Roofs were in bad condition with no division walls to the roof space. Internal services have been provided by extensions to the rear and insulation and central heating provided.

The street facade has been cleaned, new roofs, windows and doors provided along with the closure of the street to traffic. Overhead electricity supplies have been undergrounded and planting introduced. This was a straightforward scheme which developed the basic character of these houses and which unified their appearance.

A great part of this village was revitalised and improved as part of a major programme and this small single-storey eighteenth-century cottage—one wing only of a 'cross' of agricultural buildings—was extended into the main group of buildings and one other wing was demolished. This demolition enabled daylighting to be provided to the central section, where a new bathroom and bedroom were provided. The project also involved a great deal of structural and roof repair, making good stone walls after demolition and the insertion of new bar-divided sash windows. The care with which this has been done has resulted in the retention and extension of the basic rural character of the cottage without any fussiness. The original stone slabs of the roof were relaid with an improved fixing technique and services were introduced. The low ceiling heights of many of the cottages was accepted and a new communal television aerial for the village has been erected hidden in high woodland. The scheme was Grant aided by the Historic Buildings Council and the Pilgrim Trust.

NUMBERS 54 and 55, FRONT STREET, TYNEMOUTH, Tyne and Wear

These two eighteenth-century terraced houses are in the town's outstanding Conservation Area and are close to the Priory and Castle. From the window of Number 57, the victorian novelist Harriet Martineau wrote of the 'commanding view from her window over the mouth of the Tyne'. These houses were in a general state of disrepair, there was dry rot present and the outbuildings were dilapidated.

The scheme undertaken provided five and six bedroom houses to modern standards, but retained as much of the original structure as possible. The extensions at the rear of the properties provide bathrooms, kitchens, bedrooms and an extension of the living rooms.

The existing street facades, windows and roof were retained, but a great deal of repair work was necessary, including replacing the entrance doors and frames to match the originals.

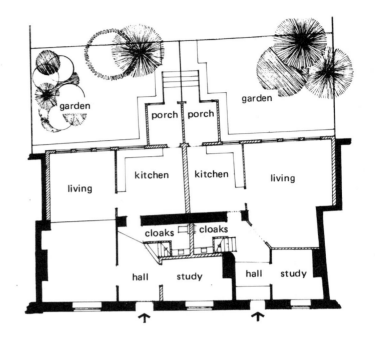

PLAN

After

Architects: Ronald F. Hall and Associates, North Shields, Tyne and Wear

This scheme reclaimed and modernised early nineteenth-century terrace houses in the western part of the city. The architecture is typical of much of the older housing of that part of the city, brick with stone dressings, string courses, cornices and doorcases. Each house has been converted into

NUMBERS 26 and 28, LANCASTER STREET, NEWCASTLE UPON TYNE

PLANS
Before

After

First Floor   Ground Floor   First Floor   Ground Floor

two self-contained flats and the attics have been stopped off. The restoration work included re-using much of the old brick and the re-creation of new matching doorcases. The front boundaries are closed by a simple metal fence and gate, and the gable wall was cleaned and rebuilt with old matching bricks. The continuing problem of whether to replace chimney stacks is well demonstrated here. Modern heating methods do not require chimneys, but their removal, particularly if this repeated throughout the street creates an arid roofline. The removal of chimneys and stacks does determine

the type of heating system and allows for no flexibility to accommodate changing supplies and costs.

The restrained re-ordering of these buildings coupled with imaginative use of existing details such as the doorcase has been carried out with considerable taste to provide good new city dwellings.

Architects: Napper Errington Collerton Partnership, Newcastle upon Tyne

Numbers 26 and 28 Lancaster Street, Newcastle upon Tyne
Above: Before and Below: After conversion

CARR HOUSE, GREAT BAVINGTON,
Northumberland

A simple but effective restoration and conversion scheme for this Northumbrian stone cottage in a remote hamlet. Above: Before and Below: After conversion

OLD FARMHOUSE, SCHOOL AYCLIFFE, County Durham

This 17th-century farmhouse is on the edge of a northern New Town, and was before purchase and restoration, in a ruinous state. The work has been sensibly limited to deal with the existing structure, to repair this and introduce modest changes. The roof had to be completely removed and replaced and there was much work to stonefacings, cracked lintols, etc. Rendering was removed from the wall surfaces and new services introduced

Before

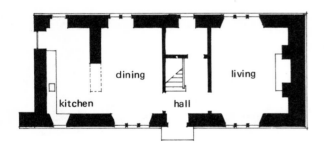

PLAN

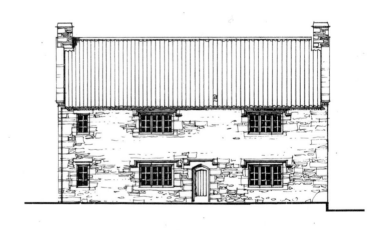

ELEVATIONS

After

36–44 WEST END, TWEEDMOUTH AND 2, 3 and 4, BLAKEWELL LANE, TWEEDMOUTH, BERWICK-UPON-TWEED, Northumberland

These pre-1850 houses are set around and close to West End, Tweedmouth, that part of the historic town of Berwick-upon-Tweed which lies to the south of the river, between Stephenson's Royal Border Bridge and the inter-war concrete Royal Tweed Bridge. Originally West End, an open green space which leads to the river lead directly to the old Berwick Bridge, and formed one of the southern exits to the town. Like much of the traditional architecture of Berwick these houses have a strong Scottish character, harled or rendered stone walls or stone built with dressed stone frontages, and with roofs either pantiled or slated. Their condition prior to renovation was very poor; substandard sanitary accommodation and cooking facilities, much rising damp and partly ruinous.

The work included the erection of rear extensions to house new services, the insertion of damp proof courses, the rearrangement of internal spaces together with the complete renewal of roof coverings and the replacement of doors and windows. This work has saved an important visual element in the scenery of the town and has provided good new homes. The basic character of the buildings has not been marred and the new extensions, carried out in a thoroughly-modern fashion, marry in splendidly.

Housing improvement at Tweedmouth. Berwick-upon-Tweed for Berwick Borough Council

Above: before and Below: after, Architects: Reavell and Cahill, Berwick-upon-Tweed

NUMBERS 12 and 13, QUAY WALLS, BERWICK-UPON-TWEED, Northumberland

Berwick town is rich in fine 18th- and 19th-century houses, many of which have, over the years, suffered from decay and neglect. To deal with this situation a Berwick Preservation Trust was formed and has started to restore and improve these houses. The first scheme was for two properties in an important position flanking the town's Quay Walls

Above: Before and Below: After restoration and conversion

Architects: Reavell and Cahill, Berwick-upon-Tweed, Northumberland

Many larger houses can be successfully divided into separate dwellings, particularly when like this house at Hutton Lowcross Park, Guisborough, Cleveland, they are long and rambling, probably with several staircases

RESTORATION

Though it is not easy to parcel schemes into those which are conversions, those which are restorations and those which are new works—almost every improvement project contains elements of each—there are some schemes where the principal objective is the restoration of the building as it stands.

The difficult question is to what stage in its life do you restore the building, to what style or period of architecture. To restore for instance a stately home, built all of a piece and by some celebrated architect, one must obviously try to get back to the original complete idea and conception. Humbler homes grew, expanded, changed and were rewindowed as family conditions, prosperity and fashions changed. Therefore what may have started out life in the seventeenth century as a typically prosperous small manor or farmhouse complete with mullioned and transomed windows, and all the trappings of the time, may well have been reglazed with Georgian sashes in the mid eighteenth century, and may have had a Victorian bay and Gothic porch added in the nineteenth. To what then should the restorer aim; the state of the house in 1850, 1750, or 1650. Obviously whatever he or she decides will have to accommodate all the necessities of modern life.

To start to scrape and return every historic building back to its original does tend to remove much of its charm, inconsequentiality and the interest that the building has acquired through age, use and even modification. The elements which intrude—the sore thumbs—should go, but be very careful in the quest for the original state of the building unless this is

very good in itself. The Edwardian bay which disrupts the orderly pattern of sash windows in a facade should go to restore the pattern and the regularity of the frontage; the Georgian sash windows in the Jacobean farmhouse should perhaps stay. As with every advice in this book, each case and each building must be considered on its own merits and the 'genius loci' acknowledged.

Restoration is perhaps the costliest of the building processes even though modern substitutes can sometimes be found; a fibre glass cornice or finial to replace ones of wood or stone, and restoration relies heavily upon the traditional craft techniques of mason, builder, joiner, carpenter and leadworker. This is where the specialist building firm—for large works—and the small firm, with a residue of tradesmen versed in the traditional techniques can score.

Traditional techniques of construction and of execution lasted longer in the country and it is often easier to find appropriate craftsmen there than in many large cities.

Restoration implies some scholarship on the part of both client and architect. Research into the documentation of the building, old drawings, conveyances and plans, old photographs of the building or its neighbourhood even perhaps written or published descriptions. In some counties, the Royal Commission on Ancient and Historical Monuments Inventories contain detailed descriptions of most of the surviving earlier houses and cottages—Westmorland is a good example of this. In any case, investigate your local Records Office, ask old inhabitants of the area or the local historian or historical society. Find out if the building is included on the List of Historic Buildings compiled by the Department of the Environment—your local Planning Office or Library should be able to tell you. This will, if the building is listed, include a short description of the house and some indication of its date. There are several routes to determining the age of a building, town maps and the Ordnance Survey are sometimes useful.

There are other seemingly easy ways to determine the age of the building or of parts of the building, incised dates and initials over doors and on tablets; the size of the materials, bricks for example were of exceptionally large size during the period of the tax on bricks, levied by number employed from 1784 to 1850; by other factual dating such as lead hopper heads, though these should be treated with caution since

NUMBER 83, MICKLEGATE, YORK

A restoration and conversion of a small but important late 17th-century townhouse in York. The scheme included improvements to the rear and the yard, and the rescue of this building from its delapidated condition. Great care was taken to bring back the original condition of the brickwork and pointing which involved the removal of numerous layers of paint. The interior was upgraded and ugly modern fireplaces were replaced. The dormer window is a very successful addition and further windows were inserted into the gable. The standard of joinery restoration is very high—see page 83

Architects: Tom Adams Design Associates, York

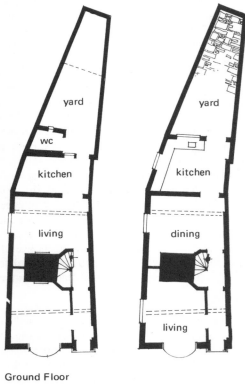

Ground Floor

BEFORE   AFTER

A conversion of two brick and pantile agricultural cottages to form student's lodgings at the University of York. Apart from some plan alterations, new windows and glazing have been inserted. One of the most important changes is in the landscaping and setting of the cottages; one side fronts the village street while the other faces the remains of an old orchard. Here the overgrown and wild 'garden' has been tamed with some hard surfacing and grass whilst keeping the most important trees and walls.

Architects: York University Design Unit, York

EDEN'S COTTAGE AND SYCAMORE COTTAGE, HESLINGTON, YORK

many were put up to comply with the local enforcement of Acts of Parliament requiring adequate guttering in towns; of from internal dating on fittings, panelling, etc. These latter items were however moved from house to house and incorporated into later rebuildings and should be regarded with caution.

The sensitivity and scholarship of the architect involved in restoration work is of paramount importance and should be considered when looking for an architect to supervise a restoration project. There are however pattern books and other information publications now available and these are summarised in the bibliography.

WHITFIELD PLACE, WOLSINGHAM, County Durham

Architect: J. D. Telfer RIBA

Wolsingham is an attractive small market town in the Pennines section of the valley of the River Wear. It is a town of gritstone and stone-slabbed roofs arranged around the central open Market Place. Whitfield Place was originally three houses, and at one time formed the Pack Horse Inn. Its exterior has remained much as was originally built in 1677 in a provincial Jacobean style with small mullioned casements and bay windows with over-swept roofs. It is set prettily facing a cobbled forecourt along the main street of the town and is flanked by handsome early eighteenth-century houses. Local tradition has it that Charles II rode up the main stairs—which survive—on horseback.

In 1971 the group was seriously dilapidated and the task of restoration and improvement began with new owners. A damp-proof course was inserted and the structure treated for woodworm. The whole of the stone-slabbed roof had to be relayed and some new roof timbers incorporated. During the restoration some of the original stone fireplaces were revealed and features such as the panelling of some rooms and oak beams renewed and repaired. A small link was constructed at the rear to provide for the rearrangement of rooms. This and the new servicing have been expertly and deftly integrated with the old structure and harmonise well without being overtly 'period'.

It was an ambitious rescue operation; eighteenth- and nineteenth-century doors were retained together with their door furniture and other interior features protected and preserved—on opening out one old fireplace, a salt cupboard was found in the wall.

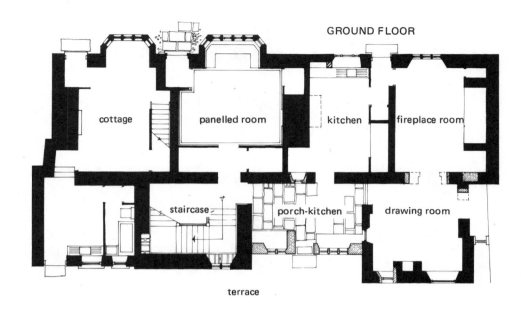

GROUND FLOOR

cottage   panelled room   kitchen   fireplace room

staircase   porch-kitchen   drawing room

terrace

PLANS

After

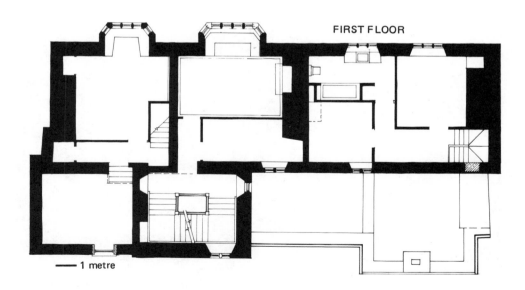

FIRST FLOOR

1 metre

Above left: Whitfield Place from the village street, before
Left: . . . after completion of restoration work
Above: The decorative date stone

The Old Hall from the south east, before restoration

Architect and owner: J. A. G. Niven

THE OLD HALL, WEST AUCKLAND,
County Durham

bath

st

bedroom   living   study

bath

bedroom   bedroom   bedroom

First Floor

PLANS

After

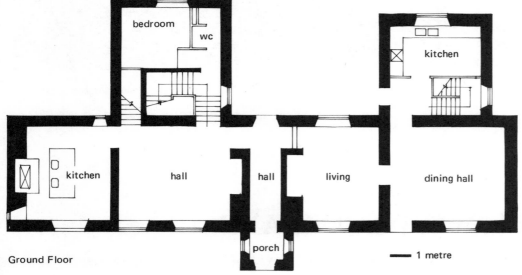

bedroom   wc

kitchen

kitchen   hall   hall   living   dining hall

porch

Ground Floor

— 1 metre

Late 17th-century oak staircase at the Old Hall, West Auckland, County Durham, retained and restored

The restoration and refurbishing of old houses is not only the province of the wealthy; this fine and important early seventeenth-century house was taken on by young people. The building was stripped almost to its basic structure, the stone walls repaired and repointed, new stone chimneys built and some of the original windows replaced. The block was completely reroofed with handmade clay pantiles, and new leaded casement windows inserted. Inside, there is much work still to do, although existing features, including a splendid original staircase have been retained and old fireplaces have been uncovered and opened up. Some of the original roof trusses, which were too rotten to retain, have been replaced by others from a local barn.

THE OLD HALL, WEST AUCKLAND, County Durham

Above and left: The Old Hall, West Auckland after completion of restoration work. The pointing of old masonry can change the overall character of the building

Joinery detail needs careful and scholarly restoration. The 18th-century doorcase of 83 Micklegate, York, before and after restoration
Contractors: William Anelay Limited, Osbaldwick, York

KEELMAN'S HOSPITAL, NEWCASTLE UPON TYNE

View from City Road before restoration and conversion

Architects: Ronald Chipchase and Partners, Newcastle upon Tyne

This ancient and historic group is close to the centre of the city. Established and built in 1701 as a hospital for the 'Keelmen' of the Tyne it stands above City Road and is a remarkable early brick structure grouped around a plain quadrangle, with decorative 'Dutch' dormers and a clock tower and cupola. After several years of disuse and decay, it has been well restored to provide housing accommodation for students at Newcastle University. Although this accommodation is perhaps neither house nor cottage, the scheme does show how old buildings of many types and previous uses can be restored and converted to provide accommodation, flats, etc.

The fine stone house dates from 1715 when it was built by Francis Rudston, Mayor of Newcastle. It was a house of some importance until the nearby town of Gateshead began to spread as a result of the growth along the Tyne during the early years of the Industrial Revolution. By 1839 it had become a school—the Crow Hall Academy. Though it was to become a house again, by the early years of this century it had been subdivided into tenements. The present owners took over the building when severe structural decay cast doubts over its future and they inaugurated a programme of restoration. Originally probably of only two storeys, the most urgent task was to completely take down the main facade, which was parting from the rest of the structure, and rebuild this. The subdivisions internally were removed to restore the original layout.

The brick-built attached wing to the west of the house was also restored and separated to become a self-contained cottage.

An early 18th-century house, now surrounded by housing estates. The house had been neglected and divided into tenements. Visual records of the house go back to 1839, and until 1847 it served as an Academy. Probably originally of only two storeys, the front walls were severly bowed and the present owner has so far concentrated much of his efforts on stabilising the main facade and structure

Above left: Crow Hall in 1939, and Below left: today

CROW HALL, FELLING, GATESHEAD, Tyne and Wear

HOUSES FROM BARNS

A great deal of interest has been shown in recent years in creating houses from other buildings and this section of the book describes some of the more successful of these conversions.

Firstly, houses from agricultural buildings, stables, barns, byres, etc. These have, in the main, one great asset—they are generally in idyllic rural settings, and although there are many planning objections to their conversion and the ensuant creation of housing within otherwise open countryside or in areas like Green Belts, there have been a good many carried through. The wit and flair of the designer is of great importance particularly in matters such as the insertion of windows into barns for these are usually structures which may have one or more large doors and that is all. The insertion of many windows, necessary to a house as such may make the building look fussy and the simple bold lines of the building lost. Other problems are those of providing adequate ceiling heights if the building is to be divided into two storeys; the provision of appropriate and harmonious extensions; providing services—electricity, water, drainage, etc., if the property is isolated and of access roads and tracks. These mean that what is really being taken on is in many cases only a structural shell, and if the roof has to be renewed, then it is simply four walls. Nevertheless, even given all the obstacles and the resulting costs, conversion of a barn or an agricultural building may, as well as providing a good house, ensure the continuity of a fine building which might otherwise have decayed and eventually disappeared.

Some rural areas rely, for the quality and interest of their landscape, upon field barns; Wensleydale for example, has an almost unparalleled collection of magnificent stone-built barns in almost every field.

Secondly other buildings such as cowbyres—shippons in Cumbria—or stables provide excellent opportunities, provided that the conversion is handled deftly and again respects the basic structure. In many cases, stables survive as the only elements of once great houses, and where these are large or based around a courtyard, may be suitable subjects for conversion into a group of houses.

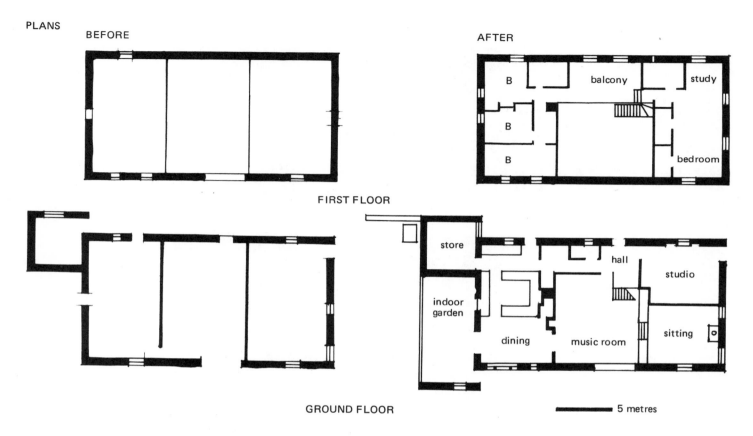

PLANS

BEFORE

AFTER

FIRST FLOOR

B

balcony

study

B

B

bedroom

GROUND FLOOR

store

indoor garden

hall

studio

dining

music room

sitting

5 metres

Architects: Wales, Wales and Rawson, Skipton, North Yorkshire

CHURCH GATE FARM, THORNTHWAITE, HARROGATE, North Yorkshire

One of the best examples of how a simple sturdy Northern Barn should be converted to form a house for today. The character—the two-storey arched doorway opening, the assymetrical window and door openings and the interior with its great truss beams—is not only retained, but, with great imagination, employed to give the new owners a home entirely fitting their special needs. The use of dark paintwork and the lightness of the glazing divisions retains the strong shapes of the various openings and contrasts well with the restored masonry. The barn, which dates from the early nineteenth century, was unused and sited close to an existing farm. All the existing window and door openings were re-used together with seven newly-formed openings and a new conservatory was provided.

87

Barn at Thornthwaite, North Yorkshire. The barns of the Yorkshire Dales have a strong form and local identity, not easily translated into a dwelling house. Successful schemes introduce few new openings and retain the strong shapes of those already there. Left: Before work and Below: After

A simple and successful conversion of disused farm buildings at Muckley, Northumberland. Architect: John Cameron RIBA Right: Before conversion and Below right: After

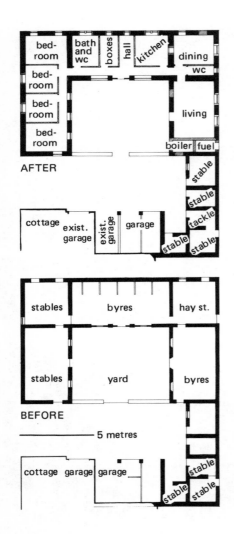

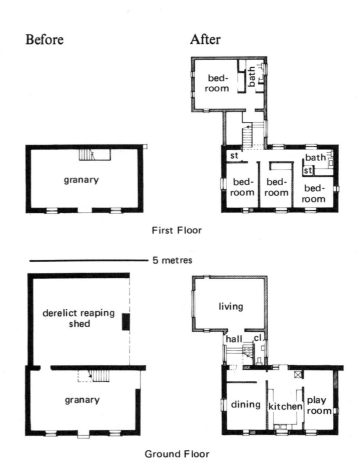

Before

After

First Floor

5 metres

Ground Floor

STABLES, BLAGDON HALL, Northumberland

A sympathetic conversion of a disused stone-built stable block to form a one-storey house. Designers: Blagdon Estates

OLD GRANARY, LITTLETHORPE, Easington, County Durham

An old-stone Granary with a new extension, converted to form a medium-sized house

90

PARK HOUSE, MIDDLETON, Northumberland

A splendid though expensive conversion of an existing cottage, previously subdivided, and outbuildings. New windows and doors, surrounding landscaping and the restoration of the fabric were all carried out with great taste and sensitivity. New elements look as though they have always belonged and are a continuing part of the vernacular tradition

PLANS

BEFORE

byres

k.2   hall

living 1   living 2

5 metres

AFTER

fuel   garage   boiler   kitchen   dining   hall   living

st

cloaks   study

Architects: Mauchlen, Weightman and Elphick, Newcastle upon Tyne

Park House, Middleton, Northumberland. Above: After conversion and Left: Before

THE BARN, WEST WITTON, North Yorkshire

Two Wensleydale barn conversions of great taste and imagination. The use of modern windows and elements, aided by the recession of these from the wall face, produces a modern look to these buildings whilst still retaining the 'country' character

Architects: Gill, Dockray Rhodes and Moore, Kendal, Cumbria

CHAPEL HOUSE, CARPERBY, North Yorkshire

PENBERTH HOUSE, KILLINGWORTH, Tyne and Wear

A brilliant and practical conversion of disused farm buildings in the middle of a New Town. Modern detailing combines with the retention of the old barn and roof to produce a sophisticated house for today

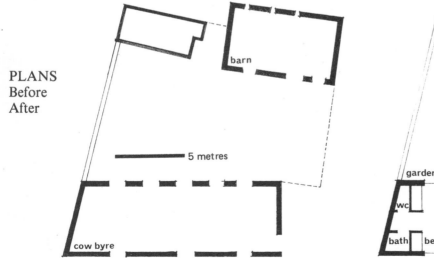

PLANS
Before
After

barn

5 metres

cow byre

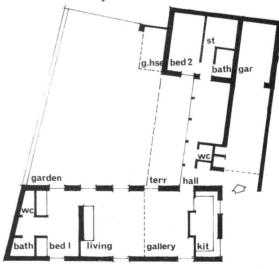

st

g.hse bed 2

bath gar

wc

garden terr hall

wc

bath bed I living gallery kit

Architects: Ainsworth Spark Associates, Newcastle upon Tyne

OTHER BUILDINGS

One of the most pressing problems facing the conservation movement today in providing a future for old and sometimes historic buildings, is to find new uses for buildings whose original purposes have disappeared or which are surplus to the present day requirements of a community. The range of such buildings is wide and includes abandoned churches, chapels, schools, industrial buildings—mills, warehouses and so on. One happy knack of the human race is that provided a building, or rooms within it, are dry, warm, comfortable, have modern requirements of servicing and are reasonably convenient, then people and in particular families can turn them into suitable homes. In a way the human being is, in terms of his immediate environment, infinitely versatile. Many examples exist of houses and flats in old warehouses, mills, country chapels even extreme subjects such as disused telephone exchanges, rural slaughterhouses, smithies and railway stations. Nowhere is impossible provided the possibilities and the inherent character of the structure are exploited; a pretty Victorian railway station complete with elegant railway Gothick stonework, windows and doors, decorative timber bargeboards and a platform, fronting a disused line where the track has been taken up in a rural situation, is a combination of good site, good building and the potential for an excellent family home. The other benefit of course is, given due respect and treatment of the building, the retention of a building of character which would otherwise disappear.

The problems of approval, servicing and site vary from example to example, but as many of these subjects have already contained some elements of housing, these are not generally insurmountable.

Interior of principal room, converted Barn at Thornthwaite, North Yorkshire

96

Conversion and extension of a derelict Windmill, orginally built about 1500, at the Thruff, Shield Green, Hexham, Northumberland. A Dining—Entrance room, kitchen, cloakroom and garage are in the new extension, whilst the restored windmill contains the living room, bathroom and bedrooms

Architects: William Gowar and Partners, Newcastle upon Tyne

INTERIORS

Although this book is devoted primarily to the external good looks of houses and cottages, some word and thought should be given to what we do to the interiors of these buildings. The cottage 'interior' is an emotive a concept as that of the cottage and its place in the landscape or countryside; nooksy, low beamed rooms, small and deeply set windows, large open wood fires are rooted in almost everyone's subconscious. Rarely do interiors live up to what we imagine them to be. Only very occasionally in restoring an old house does one find, on removing the hardboard lining to the walls of a room, fine oak panelling beneath or when rooting out a crude thirties tiled fireplace discover intact an ancient stone fireplace. Nevertheless, such things and discoveries do occur. One must always be prepared for the unexpected in dealing with old buildings, the pleasant as well as the disastrous.

Interiors are extremely vulnerable to changing fashion and fancy as well as improved standards of heating, lighting and general environment. Even now, the first action of many new owners is to remove old victorian marble fireplace surrounds, to scrape away the elaborate plaster cornices of that age and to box in with boarding the turned balusters of the staircase. This is more than a personal statement and one which accepts the 'period' trappings only so long as they do not influence the modernism of the rooms. Without flair and a highly developed and imaginative design sense, these actions almost invariably result in rooms with no character whatsoever, as bland and boring as a cardboard box. It has been frequently and capably demonstrated how old furniture can live amicably and gracefully alongside the best of today's design, so too with the overall interior design concept.

The way in which the interior design of the house or cottage takes shape depends on many factors:

how much of what is already there can be kept

how retained features, the shape, form and lighting of the spaces can become part of what is the overall aim

how new spaces can be created in conversions such as industrial buildings, agricultural buildings, etc.

what character and layout present fittings, furniture, fabrics and carpets will give to the spaces when transferred there

Lighting is a most important factor and a modern technique which can amplify and enhance spaces within old buildings. But of course, there are many other considerations; heating—what form it will take to accommodate the various fittings necessary for an old building; floor and wall finishes suitable to the situation, use, wear and general character of the building. Nowhere does changing fashion in these and the other items control interior design more apparently than in the kitchen. The pendulum of fashion has already swung from the ultra hygienic steel and ceramic surfaced kitchens of the fifties and sixties, to the folksy, humanised farmhouse-type kitchens complete with stripped pine, knotty boarding and natural finishes of today and in converting or restoring an old house, full vent can be given to these fashionable ideas.

Rooms, like the complete house, are a major investment in our lives, and the selection of carefully thought out aims towards a suitable character are best given thorough consideration. From the setting down of these ideas, the choice of elements appropriate to the overall plan will follow.

Provided that really major structural changes are not involved and that good original features are not destroyed or removed, interior design is a somewhat transitory art and can reflect the ideas, fashions and tastes of the owners to embody the ideas of their age group, background and education. Without this freedom to work within the framework of the old house and its personality, individual personality and vitality will be lost. In short, don't be afraid to experiment, provided that the experiment and its results are capable of easy remedy.

BUILDING
AND THE LAW

Statutory procedures apply to almost every item of building work and in addition to those governing new building work, there are others related directly to buildings listed by the Department of the Environment as being of architectural importance or historic interest.

Firstly, there is the question of planning permission which is requires when 'development' in the legal sense is undertaken. Development is defined in planning law as 'the carrying out of building, engineering or mining or other operations in, on, over or under the land, or the making of any material change in the use of building or other land'. Any activity therefore requires planning permission unless it is specifically excluded, although some permissions may be automatically given in orders or regulations made under the main Act. The 1971 Act specifies six activities which do not constitute development and therefore do not require any kind of planning permission. The conditions from this Act which directly apply to the alteration or conversion of houses are as follows:

(a) The maintenance, improvement or alteration of any building which affects only the interior, and does not materially affect the external appearance provided that it is not making good war damage and does not involve providing more space below ground.

(b) The use of any building or land within the curtilage of the dwelling house for any purpose incidental to the enjoyment of the house—this does not include erecting a building.

However a material change of use is specified in the case of the use as two or more separate dwelling houses of a building previously used as a single dwelling.

The General Development Order gives automatic permission for twenty-three classes of 'permitted development'. These include many kinds of small improvements and extensions to houses, but these can be brought under the Local Authorities control by making directions under Article 4 of the order. Some such directions require the approval of the Secretary of State although Local Authorities might invoke this procedure in a Conservation Area. The Development Control system is currently under review and the Final Report (February 1975) describes what, to many, must be one of the most indigestable facts of the system—delays. It says 'House builders, however, often have good reason to resent delays to their detailed applications. Control in practice is generally exercised by laymen whose ill-founded pernicketiness may be out of proportion to a detail's importance. Parkinson's Law applies here; the committee which swallows an outsize camel may strain inordinately at the gnat of detail.' Nevertheless, in buildings of the scale and size of most cottages and houses, detail is what matters and much of what is allowed as of 'permitted development'—new windows in an ancient building, a new concrete garage alongside a fine brick house, can be visually destructive even if legally permissible.

In addition to the procedure of obtaining planning permission, permission is required for all building works under the Building Regulations. These came into effect in February 1966 and replaced the somewhat haphazard system of local building by-laws set up under the Public Health Act 1936. The complex document covers all aspects of the construction and fitness of the building—materials used, protection of walls, roofs, damp and weather resistance, thermal insulation, minimum areas of rooms, ceiling heights, areas of fixed and openable glazing, etc. The amateur, planning an apparently simple scheme of improvements can soon fall foul of these regulations—for example by planning a staircase which is steeper than permitted or without the required headroom or by planning to use roof space which requires fresh joists across or does not comply with the fire regulations. It is in this field that the expertise and knowledge of the architect can be most useful. Some of the regulations are difficult to incorporate into old buildings and may seem somewhat arbitrary; ceiling heights are a good example. In these cases it is worth considering an application to the Local Authority for a relaxation of the regulations in part, particularly if one is dealing with a listed building. The Royal Institute of British Architects can supply information on the relaxation of Building Regulations citing examples.

Good conversions bring the best of modern improvements to join the best of what already exists. Cottage character retained at Twistleton's Yard, Settle, North Yorkshire

Where however good features remain, like this 18th-century panelling at Hide Hill, Berwick-upon-Tweed, then it should be retained and restored

Where nothing exists a sympathetic modern interior has to be created. Penberth House, Killingworth, Tyne and Wear

LISTED BUILDINGS

Prior to 1944 there existed no provision in the British statutes for protecting inhabited dwellings of historic or architectural interest. What preservation measures that existed then were embodied in the various Ancient Monuments Acts which were concerned with sites or uninhabited buildings which by reason of their historical, architectural, traditional, artistic or archaeological interest were of public concern. The 1944 Town & Country Planning Act marked a change of attitude about the importance of buildings and provisions were introduced which required the then Minister of Town & Country Planning to compile a list of buildings of special architectural or historical interest.

The principles for selection and inclusion in the lists were drawn up by an expert committee of architects, antiquaries and historians and these principles are, in general, still followed. All buildings built before 1700 which survive in anything like their original condition are listed. Most buildings dating from the period 1700 to 1840 are also listed though selection is necessary, while buildings from the Victorian and Edwardian era are only considered suitable for inclusion if they have a definite quality and character (and really the selection is designed merely to include the principal works of the principal architects of the period). In addition certain buildings are now also included which date from the inter-war period. In choosing buildings particular attention is paid to four factors:

1. Good examples of architectural style, pieces of planning or good illustrations of social or economic history.
2. Technical innovations.
3. Association with well-known characters or events.
4. Group value, as it is now recognised that individual buildings of little architectural interest may combine together into important groups.

The original listing for the whole country was completed in 1968 and the buildings were classified into three grades.

GRADE I consists of buildings considered to be of such outstanding importance that only the greatest necessity would justify their demolition and consists of only a small percentage of the total number listed.

GRADE II buildings are those considered to be of considerable historic or architectural importance and which have a good claim to survive. Some particularly important buildings in this category are classified as GRADE II*.

The third category of classification GRADE III buildings did not normally qualify for inclusion in the statutory lists but were considered important enough to be drawn to the attention of local authorities. Since 1970 the concept of Grade III, or supplementary list, buildings has been abandoned and many of the buildings formally included in this category have been elevated to Grade II standard. The types of buildings that have been so treated are detailed in the appendix of Department of the Environment Circular 102/74.

The fact that a building is listed as of special interest does not necessarily mean that it will be preserved untouched in all circumstances but it does demand that a strong case be made for demolition. As the Department of the Environment Circular 61/68 points out 'The destruction of listed buildings is very seldom necessary for the sake of improvement; more often it is the result of a failure to appreciate good architecture'. The statutory lists therefore provide a guide to the heritage of buildings that are all around. These statutory lists of buildings are therefore important and provision to enable the public to inspect the list for their particular areas is made at local planning departments or alternatively they can all be consulted at the National Monuments Record, Fortress House, 23 Saville Row, London W1X 1AB.

Originally little statutory protection was provided for listed buildings apart from the power the local authority had to apply building preservation orders. This, however, was all changed by Section V of the 1968 Town & Country Planning Act which introduced Listed Building Consent. The previous system of control by means of building preservation orders was abolished. Instead the demolition or the alteration or extension of any building which is on a statutory list now requires consent, and the Secretary of State has issued a set of criteria to give broad guidance to local planning authorities in dealing with such applications. They are asked to consider:

1. The importance of the building both intrinsically and relatively to other special buildings in the area (the building may be important either individually or because of its contribution to the total townscape.)
2. The architectural merit and historical interest of the

particular building.

3. Its condition, the cost of repair and maintaining it in relation to its importance and whether any grant is available.

4. The importance of any alternative use for the site and in particular whether the use of the site for some public purpose would make it possible to enhance the environment and especially to enhance other listed buildings in the area.

The 1971 Town & Country Planning Act which has absorbed most of the previous legislation also imposes a number of other requirements, notably the publicising of the applications, making provisions to enable a local planning authority to serve a 'repairs notice' and insisting that the Department of the Environment be informed so that they might consider whether to call in an application for decision at central government level. In addition to the 1971 Act there are a number of other Acts that relate to listed buildings. In particular the Local Authorities (Historic Buildings) Act 1962 provides a discretionary right to local authorities to make grants towards the preservation and repair of buildings included on the statutory list.

CONSERVATION AREAS

The Department of the Environment Circular 53/67 made four points that a planning authority should observe when dealing with Conservation Areas and the buildings therein:

   (i) Special attention should be paid to the objectives of conversion when exercising any functions under the various provisions of the Planning Acts, especially with regard to the desirability of preserving or enhancing the quality or character of the particular area.

  (ii) There should be a shift away from a negative control to creative planning.

 (iii) Designation should be regarded as a preliminary to action and not to end in its own right.

  (iv) The ultimate aim should be the production of a positive policy for each Conservation Area.

The last point is especially important and it was suggested that any effective policy should touch on three aspects: control of development, preservation and improvement. Many of the points made in Circular 53/67 have been extended by subsequent legislation.

Control of Development

Clearly the basic tenet of the policy for any area must be one of control rather than prevention for it is essential not to fossilise Conservation Areas—museum pieces are alright in their place but cannot generally be considered as acceptable parts of a living community. This being the case the standard of any new development (whether it be a new building or an alteration to an existing one) is crucial.

The Town and Country Amenities Act 1974 has also changed the law relating to trees in Conservation Areas. Now anyone, intending to cut down, top, lop, uproot, wilfully damage or wilfully destroy any tree inside a Conservation Area, must give the relevant district council six weeks notice of his intention, so as to give them time to consider the desirability or otherwise of making a tree preservation order before the work proposed is carried out.

Other requirements include the posting of site notices and the advertisement of any development which might adversely affect the character of a Conservation Area.

Preservation

The importance of listed buildings to any particular Conservation Area is obvious and usually, in development control, the presumption is considered to be in favour of preservation unless a strong case can be made to the contrary. Similarly Local Authorities are urged to make greater use of their enforcement powers, particularly as regards compulsory purchase and the serving of repairs notices. Section 6 of the Town and Country Amenities Act 1974 means that a Local Authority, desiring to compulsorily purchase a listed building, will no longer have to pay the redevelopment value of the site and should therefore have to pay less to acquire it. Another provision of the same Act has empowered Local Authorities to secure the repair of unoccupied buildings in the Conservation Area and given other powers to obtain the money from the owner without the ultimate recourse of having to compulsorily purchase the building. Provision has also been made to protect unlisted buildings sited within the prescribed boundaries of a Conservation Area by applying, with modifications, the listed building control provisions. Section 277A means that no building (with a few minor exceptions—contained in paragraph 15 of Circular 147/74) can be demolished or even partially demolished without permission.

Improvement

In the 117 Conservation Areas that have been classed as 'outstanding' by the Historic Buildings Council (1975), it is possible for the local authority to make use of substantial funds from central government to promote improvement works. One particularly popular method has been the Town Scheme. Circular 86/72 details the financial assistance available from central government. In the other areas the Local Planning Authority can set an example by the replacement, where necessary, of unsuitable (or ill-sited) public equipment and fixtures.

The term 'Conservation Area' has a specific statutory definition which appeared with the introduction of the Civic Amenities Act in 1967. Before this date, legislation provisions had been concerned merely to protect individual buildings of merit or indeed often just to bring the existence of such building to the attention of the Planning Authorities. The move from a building to an area basis was in recognition of the growing awareness of the desirability of considering the environment as a whole and also the need for greater concerted action in general. The definition occurred in section 1(1) which is now incorporated in section 277 of the Town and Country Planning Act 1971 (as amended by the Town and Country Amenities Act 1974). It says: 'Every Local Planning Authority shall from time to time determine which parts of their area are areas of special architectural or historic interest, the character or appearance of which is desirable to preserve or enhance and shall designate such areas.'

Thus, whilst every building within a Conservation Area now has statutory protection, most cottages, farmhouses, etc., outside these areas fall outside the scope of present listings. Some vernacular buildings may be included on the Grade III lists. Any action which may cause 'damage' to a listed building is punishable by a fine of up to £100, and £20 per day until steps are taken to prevent further damage. The fact that a building is listed does not mean that it will be preserved intact in all circumstances, but it does mean that demolition must not be allowed unless the case for it has been fully examined and that alterations must preserve that character of the building as far as possible. If the owner claims that the building has become incapable of reasonably beneficial use in its present state, and its alteration is opposed by the Local Authority, he may serve a Listed Building Purchase Notice. It is not a question however of whether it is of less use in its present state than if developed. The accent is always on conservation.

These few notes on some of the statutory procedures involved before building works are undertaken are only a brief summary of the present legislation and they cannot supersede the need for qualified legal or technical advice.

GRANTS

Local Authorities administer and give grants—standard and discretionary—towards modernisation and improvement schemes. The standard grant provides a house for the first time with basic amenities—basin, sink, hot and cold water supply, bath or shower and flush lavatory. The grant is generally half of the cost up to a maximum, or this can be extended towards further building to house these. These grants must be applied for and approved of before any building work takes place so that the seeking of grant approval forms another task to be undertaken when Building Regulation and planning approvals are sought.

Discretionary grants are not as of right and are for substantial improvement to bring the property to a high standard. The Local Authorities contribution may be up to one half of the cost, though this may also be extended by loans. As the grants are designed primarily for the modernisation of older property, extensions which simply provide more liveable space, will probably not qualify.

If the building is listed as of Architectural or Historic importance, grants may be available from the Historic Buildings Council towards the cost of repair and restoration. Local Authorities are also empowered to give grants or make loans for this purpose.

Above: This low stark Northumbrian cottage was 'improved' to Below. This now almost unrecognisable, all its regional character and most of its charm has gone

Above: A simple and unfortunate case of one into two won't go. This little ironstone cottage is ruined by a thinly framed, out-of-scale window

This derelict cottage has been 'saved' from demolition but its character has been unfortunately changed by stark horizontal windows. Above: Before and Below: After

Right: An assortment of the worst of the ready-made products applied to what was previously a simple artisans cottage; cement rendering marked with stonework joints, 'Tudor' door, bow window with pressed 'Bulls Eyes'

Below: A modern window in an ancient opening at the Deanery, South Church, Bishop Auckland, County Durham

WHAT NOT TO DO

It is always easier to say what not to do than describe what should be done. Nevertheless in the preceding chapters, this book has tried to provide some background to the various features and elements which shape the way our houses look. It is only when we do things to these buildings without care and sensitivity that things start to go badly wrong; to invest them with an importance which they never had or should have, to disregard what is already there of charm or merit, to impose half garbled or illiterate additions or alterations on them in the quest for neo-Georgiana or some obscure blank modernity or to change materials and finishes for some cheaper and less attractive substitute. Some wrongs can be righted, but most of the things we do in the name of progress and change are there for all time. Our houses are not stage sets to be changed continually with changing, often short lived, fashion; today's bright kitsch quickly becomes tomorrow's yawn. They are our homes and a formidable part of this country's heritage.

'What not to do' is a cabinet of curiosities, of things which happened to old houses and cottages in the name of modernisation and progress. Some will already be regretted, some will be proud emblems of man's triumph over house. Captions are really unnecessary but are included just in case.

With the increasing trend to hark back to previous styles and fashions and the current vogue for 'Georgianisation', the manufacturers of building components have responded with a range of builders and 'do-it-yourself' products. In the main, these are a pale imitation of the real thing and most of them are poor translations of correct and scholarly Georgian design. Nevertheless, there are some of these products which might in certain circumstances be useful.

In the conversion and restoration of old property, the size of existing openings, doorways, windows, etc., means that the use of 'off-the-peg' components to replace decayed elements or insert new ones is often impossible and they will need to be purpose made, preferably copying what is already there or nearby as closely as possible. This is expensive as the complexity of these items, e.g. a properly-constructed sash window, and the standards of the eighteenth- and nineteenth-century joinery work are generally very high.

Of the items which may be useful—off-the-peg—joinery, doors, windows, etc., come first, and the first caveat is really to be as simple as possible. Resist the temptation of glossy catalogues with intricate over doors, etc., and remember the type of building, its age and character upon which they would be placed.

Simple cottage ledged braced and battened doors are available from most manufacturers; standard height of 6' 6" (1,981 mm) and up to 2' 9" wide (838 mm). Two panelled, fielded doors, are also available, in Canadian Hemlock for painting, at the same sizes from some manufacturers. These are appropriate to earlier houses and were a traditional form in more modest houses right through the eighteenth century. The modern examples available however have light sectioned framing and styles.

Georgian six-panelled doors, in a variety of proportions are widely available with raised and fielded panels, generally in hardwood but some in Douglas Fir for painting. Again only up to 2' 9" wide (838 mm). The best examples have the arrangement of 2 small upper panels, longer centre panels, a wide rail and the shorter lower panels. These, however, will be about three times the cost of the usual 15 light glazed door. Purpose-made doors will cost fifty per cent more. A variety of pseudo types, never in fact actually used are marketed under such names as 'Gothic', 'Elizabethan' as well as whole ranges of machine-carved doors in the Spanish manner. Glass fibre and plastic mouldings, applied panels are also available to ornament the humble flush door. Avoid the pseudo and aim to be as simple as possible.

Many quirky variations are also available; some include a fanlight instead of the top panels, others with a great number of small square fielded panels. These invariably are and look like pastiches of the real thing.

Many doors, internal and external are produced in hardwood to be polished. Almost all real Georgian joinery was painted, except for internal joinery in the grander houses, and the present day replacements or introductions should, wherever possible, follow this pattern.

There are several types of ready-made pilaster, over doors and types of pediments available, all designed to bring

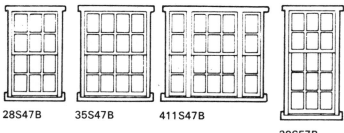

28S47B   35S47B   411S47B

28S57B

Standard sash window, available from most manufacturers, and suitable for selected situations.

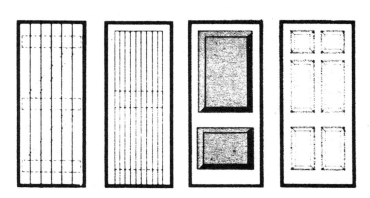

Modern windows, centre pivoted or like these examples, top hung, can be successfully used in cottage modernisation

Above top: Four basic traditional door types available currently from most manufacturers

For the replacement of grander items like door hoods, some timber examples like this are readily available

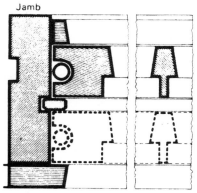

Jamb

Standard Lining

Left: Most modern sashes are spring balanced, a less troublesome technique than the old weight balances. The modern timber components lack mouldings and can again appear clumsy

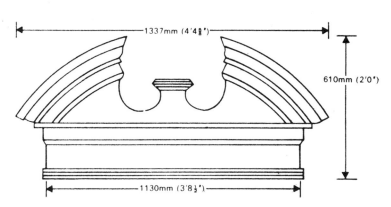

1337mm (4'4⅞")

610mm (2'0")

1130mm (3'8½")

107

A COLLECTION OF ODDITIES

Top left: An ungainly addition with an unfortunate window
Top right: One of a terrace 'improved'—new stock windows and cement
*   rendering*
Right: The three ages of 'house'—modern basic, the new 'Georgianesque'
*   and the fundamental Victorian terrace house whence all this started*

Top left: The 'Georgianised' cottage
Left: Ungainly windows and door details
Above left: Stark modern metal windows, emphasised by rendered jambs, cills and heads
Top right: Unsuited 'modernity'
Lower right: The insatiable bow window

Above: New pretentious neighbours
Above right: The village pattern of vertical windows has been ignored with nasty results
Right: Cottagification—of a simple and unpretentious cottage

Above and Below: An Edwardian villa reglazed in a simple and satisfactory way

Above: The hardness which can make the conversion of an old cottage look like an entirely new building. The very character which attracts us to older buildings can be the most devastating loss without due care at every stage of the work

Centre: The proportion of glass panes should not be overlooked. This modern insertion replaces older horizontal sliding sashes

If it has to be 'Georgian', then it should be as correct to period examples and precepts as possible. Above: A doorcase as carried out and, as it might properly have been. Even bows and bays should follow precedent

attention and importance to the doorway itself. In almost all cases, whether in timber, plastic or fibre glass, they are substitute versions of genuine detail. The eighteenth- and nineteenth-century joiner knew intimately the rules and strictures which governed classical design, or if not, could readily turn to one or more of the many pattern and design books available. These were often produced by the architects themselves, and provided either details he could copy or a sound basis upon which he could improvise. The range and variety of provincial joiners work, within the classic framework and rules is very wide. Nevertheless, they almost always conformed to the basic rules, and hence not only bear a family resemblance, but look right. Present day manufacturers' 'Georgian' is multi fit—expandable and available literally by the yard. Assemblies of these various parts to form say a cheap replacement door surround should be handled with extra care. Some are better and look better than others, but often it is the thinness of the sections and mouldings and the angle of the pediment which sets it apart as pale repro. Generally they are designed to fit the narrower doors of present day use, and hence the general proportions can be long and drawn out. If an elaborate door surround is really needed, better to replace exactly what was there, or to study one of the several books on period detailing currently available to select a model for something appropriate and suitable. If in real doubt veer towards simplicity and insert a simple modern door.

Replacing or inserting windows is a greater problem. Modern standard windows look exactly what they are; cheap, efficient and unsuitable for older properties. Faced with the problem of replacing decayed sash windows for example in an eighteenth-century cottage, what are the alternatives and cost relation.

First of course one can replace the windows exactly with purpose-made joinery. These will cost more than the other alternatives, but because they will fit exactly the openings already there, they will save eventually. They can furthermore be exact copies in detail of the existing windows; the thickness and detailing of the glazing bars for example matters very much to the overall effect of the windows.

A second alternative, if one was fortunate on the openings sizes, would be to insert modified standard double hung sash windows which are available from most manufacturers or extend the openings to fit. This is a risky process as even small changes in the size of windows in the overall pattern of fenestration will change the character of a facade substantially. The best standard windows of this kind are available in 12 or 16 light sashes, 4' 7$\frac{3}{8}$" high (1,406 mm) and 2' 8$\frac{1}{2}$" (825 mm) and 3' 5$\frac{1}{2}$" (1,054 mm) wide. Taller versions, 5' 7$\frac{3}{8}$" (1,711 mm) high are available, but the disproportion between the two sashes makes them less attractive. The chief defect of these windows, which are now spring balanced, is the crudity of the glazing bars and other mouldings. The arrangement of cover linings to the outer face means that they are most easily fitted to show a wide band around the window, like the early eighteenth-century exposed sash boxes; suitable for earlier windows, but inappropriate on later buildings. They will probably cost only sixty to seventy-five per cent of what a joiner's purpose-made window would cost but there are builders' costs in connection with the openings. Some manufacturing joiners operate a service of providing factory-made purpose-made windows and sashes.

Bar divided, casement hung, modified standard windows may be useful in rural and earlier buildings, but the effect of these is again of crude glazing bars and mouldings, making the overall effect one of heaviness and complexity. Better in these situations to look for simpler modern window types without bar divisions, casement, top hung or centrally pivoted. The end effect can be of greater simplicity and more sympathetic. In certain situations an untreated and weathered hardwood outer frame can help visually.

Metal frames are most suited to early, mullioned windows where there is no real alternative to purpose-made casements.

Many good houses have been spoiled by the insertion of modern standard windows, and although these are much cheaper than even the standard double hung sashes (by over sixty per cent), their effect can be disastrous in any property of age or merit. They are suitable and appropriate for what they were designed, viz, for inexpensive windows for mass housing.

BIBLIOGRAPHY

Materials:
Davey, N., A History of Building Materials, 1961
Clifton-Taylor, A., The Pattern of English Building, Third Ed. 1972
Innocent, C. F., The Development of English Building Construction, 1916, reprinted 1971
Salzman, L. F., Building in England down to 1540, Second Ed. 1967

Vernacular:
Barley, M. W., The English Farmhouse and Cottage
Batsford, H., and Fry, O., The English Cottage, 1938
Braun, H., The English Houses, 1962
Briggs, M. S., The English Farmhouse, 1953
Jekyll, G., and Jones, S. R., Old English Household Life, reprinted 1975
Brunskill, R. W., Illustrated Handbook of Vernacular Architecture, 1970
Turner, R., The Smaller English House
Cook, O., and Smith E., The English House through Seven Centuries, 1968
Barley, M. W., The House and Home, 1963
Walton, J., Homesteads of the Yorkshire Dales, 1947

Dating:
Harvey, J. H., Sources for the History of Houses, British Records Association, Archives and User, No. 3, 1974

Restoration and Maintenance:
Insall, D., The Care of Old Buildings Today, 1972
Architectural Press, Period Houses and Their Details
Building Research Establishment Digest, Cleaning External Surfaces of Buildings, Digest Number 113, 1972

Legal:
The New Citizen Guide to Town and Country Planning, TCPA, 1974
Cambridgeshire County Council, A Guide to Historic Buildings Law
Bigham, D. A., The Law and Administration Relating to the Protection of the Environment
Elder, A. J., The Guide to the Building Regulations

General:
Consumers Association, Extending Your House, 1971
Prizeman, J., Your House the Outside View, 1975
Cruikshank, D., and Wyld, P., London: The Art of Georgian Building, 1975
Lloyd, N., A History of the English House, 1931, reprinted 1975
Collymore, P., House Conversion and Renewal, 1976
National Home Improvement Council, Improving Your Home, 1976

SOURCES OF HELP AND ADVICE

ANCIENT MONUMENTS SOCIETY
33 Ladbroke Square, LONDON W11 3NB

ASSOCIATION FOR INDUSTRIAL ARCHAEOLOGY
Church Hill, Ironbridge, TELFORD, Salop

BRITISH ARCHAEOLOGICAL ASSOCIATION
Miss McClure, 61 Old Park Ridings, Winchmore Hill, LONDON N21 2ET

CIVIC TRUST
17 Carlton House Terrace, LONDON SW1Y 5AW

CIVIC TRUST FOR THE NORTH EAST
34/35 Saddler Street, DURHAM

CIVIC TRUST FOR THE NORTH WEST
56 Oxford Street, MANCHESTER M1 6EU

CIVIC TRUST FOR WALES
6 Park Place, CARDIFF

SCOTTISH CIVIC TRUST
24 George Square, GLASGOW G2 1EF

COUNCIL FOR BRITISH ARCHAEOLOGY
8 St. Andrew's Place, Regent's Park, LONDON NW1

COUNCIL FOR SMALL INDUSTRIES IN RURAL AREAS
11 Cowley Street, LONDON SW1

COUNCIL FOR THE PROTECTION OF RURAL ENGLAND
4 Hobart Place, LONDON SW1Y 0HY

COUNTRYSIDE COMMISSION
John Power House, Crescent Place, CHELTENHAM, Glos., GL50 3RA

DEPARTMENT OF THE ENVIRONMENT
2 Marsham Street, LONDON SW1P 3EB
(Local Offices—see local Directories)

DIRECTORATE OF ANCIENT MONUMENTS AND HISTORIC BUILDINGS
Fortress House, 23 Saville Row, LONDON W1X 2AA

HISTORIC BUILDINGS COUNCIL
25 Savile Row, LONDON W1X 2AY

MEN OF THE STONES
A. S. Ireson, Esq., The Rutlands, Tinwell, STAMFORD, Lincs.

GEORGIAN GROUP
2 Chester Street, LONDON SW1X 7BB

NATIONAL RECORD OF INDUSTRIAL MONUMENTS
University of Bath, Northgate House, Upper Bath Walls, BATH BA1 5AL

NATIONAL TRUST
42 Queen Anne's Gate, LONDON SW1H 9AS
(Local Agents Offices—see local Directories)

ROYAL COMMISSION OF HISTORIC MONUMENTS —including **NATIONAL MONUMENTS RECORD**
Fortress House, 23 Savile Row, LONDON W1X 2AA

ROYAL INSTITUTE OF BRITISH ARCHITECTS
66 Portland Place, LONDON W1N 4AD
(Local Headquarters—see local Directories)

ROYAL TOWN PLANNING INSTITUTE
26 Portland Place, LONDON W1N 4BE

SOCIETY FOR THE PROTECTION OF ANCIENT BUILDINGS
55 Great Ormond Street, LONDON WC1N 3JA

SOCIETY FOR POST MEDIEVAL ARCHAEOLOGY
Passmore Edwards Museum, Romford Road, Stratford, LONDON E15 4LZ

VICTORIAN SOCIETY
29 Exhibition Road, LONDON SW7 2AS

TOWN AND COUNTRY PLANNING ASSOCIATION
17 Carlton House Terrace, LONDON SW1Y 5AS

The modern improved cottage interior at its best. Simple, sympathetic and straighforward. Interior of Eden's Cottage, Heslington, York

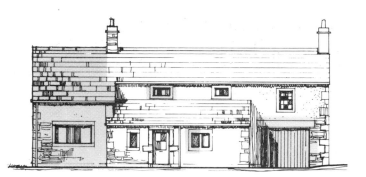

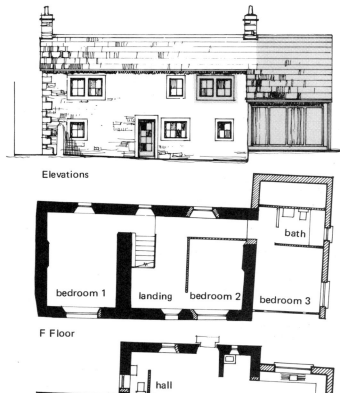

Elevations

F Floor

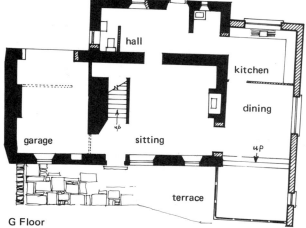

G Floor

Cottage extension at Moorview, Cracoe, North Yorkshire. A happy solution of type (g)
Architects: Wales, Wales and Rawson, Skipton, North Yorkshire

ACKNOWLEDGEMENTS

The making of this Handbook would not have been possible without the continued interest and support of the sponsors and of the large number of individuals, groups, Authorities and others who entered properties which had been improved or converted for the Award Scheme mounted by the Civic Trust for the North East in 1975. To all of these, the compilers and publishers of this book extend their sincere thanks.

Especial thanks are also extended to the various architects and surveyors who allowed their work to be included, and these are noted wherever possible throughout the book. The following photographers are gratefully acknowledged for so generously allowing their work to be used:

James Riddell: Cover, 66
Colin Westwood: Cover, 92
A. Ainslie Wilson: 6, 30, 78
Ursula Clark: 10, 34, 46
Brian Cottrell: 11
Photo Mayo: 23
Turners Ltd: 38
Jack T. Merriott: 43
Charles Crisp: 47
The Laurence Sterne Trust: 59
Keith Gibson: 88, 96
Philipson Studios: 100
National Monuments Record: 120

A final note of appreciation and thanks to the members of the Trust's staff and Board who either worked on the production of the book or who carefully read through the progressive stages in its creation and helpfully criticised and commented.

GLOSSARY OF TECHNICAL AND OTHER TERMS USED IN THIS BOOK

ARCH four centred

ARCHITRAVE

The cover moulding or surround to a door; an integral part of the doorcase. Also one of the three main parts of the entablature of a classical 'order'.

ASHLAR

Smooth-faced masonry generally of large blocks, cut to squared edges.

BOND Brickwork

English; alternate courses of the wall face are of headers and stretchers only. Flemish; alternate headers and stretchers in each row.

CORNICE

A projecting decorative element usually at the top of a wall, opening or at the eaves. Also the uppermost of the three main parts of the entablature of a classical 'order'.

CRUCK

Large curved beams supporting the roof of a house.

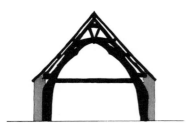

DENTILS and pendants

A decorative moulding usually a part of a classical cornice—of Roman Doric.

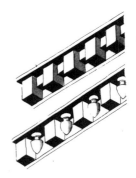

DOOR Braced and battened

A simple door of vertical timbers—battens—with cross timbers— ledges—and braces on the inner face.

ENTABLATURE

The crowning features in a classical 'order', i.e. all the horizontal elements above the column and capital.

ESCUTCHEON

The metal, ivory or other plate surrounding a keyhole or part of a lock.

FIELDED PANEL

Raised joinery panel.

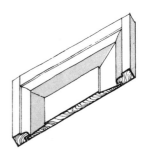

FLASHINGS

Protective leadwork or other material to roof valleys, around chimneys and other sites where differing material meet.

FRIEZE

The central feature of the three elements of the classical entablature.

GOTHICK architecture

Decorative eighteenth-century Gothic revival architecture promoted by Horace Walpole and architects of the period. In a sense the English equivalent of the continental Rococo.

HARLING

A lowland Scottish technique of rendering the outer face of the buildings, consisting of a 1:2:8 cement/lime/pebble sand mix.

HEADER

A brick laid so that only the end appears on the wall face.

HOPPER HEAD

KNEELER

The base stone of a capped gable.

LABEL MOULDS

or hood or drip.
A feature of early windows in masonry.

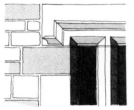

'L' HINGES

Eighteenth-century door and window hinges.

LUG or ear

The side fixings for rainwater pipes and heads, etc.

MATHEMATICAL TILES

A tile facing technique in which a uniform facing was obtained by the use of moulded tiles. The end product is virtually indistinguishable from brickwork though much lighter in weight and speedier to erect. Used only in the South East.

MOULDINGS

Planted; a moulding fixed direct to another element.

Bolection; a bold curving mould used in the seventeenth century and nineteenth century.

ORDERS

The classical basis of all Renaissance and post Renaissance arch-

itecture, comprising the column base, the column, the capital and the entablature.

PEDIMENT

A low pitched gable above a doorway, portico, window, etc.

QUOINS

Dressed stones at the angles of a building.

REVEAL

A setting back of walls or other features within their width to facilitate the setting of elements such as window frames, door cases, etc.

STRETCHER

A brick laid so that only the side face appears on the wall surface.

STRING COURSE

Projecting horizontal band or moulding set into the surface of a wall or facade.

STUCCO

Plaster facing or rendering applied to the outer walls of a building. In use from the end of the eighteenth century.

SWEPT VALLEY

A roof valley between two pitched roofs at an angle to each other in which the roofing material is carried around continuously, i.e., not stopped and joined with lead or other flashings.

VENEER

A very thin leaf of timber or other material applied to form a surface finish. Techniques of veneer cutting and hence thickness and size have changed considerably since the late seventeenth century.

VERNACULAR

The local traditional architecture or building style of an area.

VOLUTE

A spiral scroll, basically a part of the classical Ionic capital.

Our towns, villages and cities are full of the unusual and the unexpected. House and cottage conversion and improvement should aim to retain and enhance the joy and delight experienced from simply looking at these buildings

Provincial builder's 'Venetian windows' at Berwick-upon-Tweed, North-umberland. Late 18th-century